discard

X

Five Days
in London
May 1940

Books by John Lukacs

The Great Powers and Eastern Europe

Tocqueville: The European Revolution
and Correspondence with Gobineau (editor)

A History of the Cold War

Decline and Rise of Europe

A New History of the Cold War

Historical Consciousness

The Passing of the Modern Age

The Last European War, 1939–1941

1945: Year Zero

Philadelphia: Patricians and Philistines, 1900–1950

Outgrowing Democracy: A History of the
United States in the Twentieth Century

Budapest 1900: A Historical Portrait of a
City and Its Culture

Confessions of an Original Sinner

The Duel: 10 May–31 July; The Eighty-Day
Struggle Between Churchill and Hitler

The End of the Twentieth Century and the
End of the Modern Age

Destinations Past

George F. Kennan and the Origins of Containment,
1944–1946: The Kennan-Lukacs Correspondence

The Hitler of History

A Thread of Years

Five Days

in London

May 1940

John Lukacs

YALE UNIVERSITY PRESS ◆ NEW HAVEN AND LONDON

"In Westminster Abbey" is reprinted from John Betjeman,
Collected Poems, by permission of John Murray (Publishers) Ltd.

Printed in the United States of America

Library of Congress Cataloging-in-Publication Data
Lukacs, John, 1924–
Five days in London, May 1940 / John Lukacs.
p.   cm.
Includes bibliographical references (p.   ) and index.
ISBN 0-300-08030-1
1. World War, 1939–1945 — Diplomatic history.   2. World War, 1939–
1945 — Great Britain.   3. Great Britain — Politics and government —
1936–1945.   4. Halifax, Edward Frederick Lindley Wood, 1st Earl of,
1881–1959.   5. Churchill, Winston, Sir, 1874–1965.
I. Title.   II. Title: 5 days in London, May 1940.
D750.L85   1999
940.53′2 — dc21   99-27583

A catalogue record for this book is available from the British Library.

The paper in this book meets the guidelines
for permanence and durability of the Committee on Production
Guidelines for Book Longevity of the Council on Library Resources.

10   9   8   7   6   5

*This book is dedicated
to Philip and Marjorie*

Contents

Contents

Contents

Preface

My history of this history has no ascertainable origin. About forty, perhaps even fifty, years ago I was beginning to think that the last days of May in 1940 may have been decisive for the outcome of the Second World War. This idea, or thought, or perhaps not much more than a sense, accorded with my conviction that the most important phase of the Second World War was the one before December 1941, that is, before the American entry into the war, coinciding with the first German retreat before Moscow — after that, Hitler could still win great battles, but no longer the entire war. From this realization sprang my decision, in 1968, to write a rather large work, *The Last European War, 1939–1941,* eventually published in 1976. It was during this time, in 1970, that the British government chose to shorten the closed period of most of its papers, from fifty years to thirty. Accordingly I spent a few weeks in London in 1971, mostly at the Public Record Office. I may have been among the first to read and work from the PRO's cabinet papers of May–June 1940. What I read confirmed my suspicion (if that was what it was) that those days in London were very critical, and not only because of the catastrophic military situation in Flanders and in France — that Churchill's situation within the War Cabinet was much more difficult than most people, including historians at that time, thought. However, given the scope and the size and the unusual structure of *The Last European War,* I could devote not more than three pages to this, all of them in part 1, the narrative portion of the book.

Sixteen years passed, during which I wrote four or five other books, each about a different topic. In 1989 my then editor and publisher and friend John Herman, of Ticknor & Fields (now defunct), asked me what I might be thinking of writing next. I thought for a while, and said: A book about 1940 — more precisely, about the eighty days from 10 May to 31 July 1940, marked by the duel between Winston Churchill and Adolf Hitler. While writing *The Duel* I again spent a few weeks in England at the Public Record Office and at some other archives. In *The Duel* about fourteen or fifteen pages were devoted to the last week of May 1940. And then, seven years after the completion of the manuscript of *The Duel,* I chose to return to the history of those days, encouraged by the editorial director of Yale University Press, my present publishers. In 1997 and 1998 I returned to London twice for the purposes of my researches, broadened and deepened by reading in a large variety of archives and private papers. *Habent sua fata libelli:* this is the story of the present book.

Thus it may be said that this book amounts to the completion of a very lopsided trilogy: from three pages in *The Last European War* to fifteen pages in *The Duel* and then to two hundred and twenty pages in this one. Or from macrocosmic to microcosmic history, of a sort. A friend said the other day, in mock seriousness, "Will your next book be *Three Hours in London* ?" No, it won't.

I must now add a caveat. This is that not only the scope but the structures of the abovementioned books are very different. A somewhat uncategorizable historian, I am not a specialist in British political or social or military history. However, one consideration may intrude here. During the past fifteen or twenty years, British historians have written valuable articles and books dealing with Churchill and Halifax and the politics of war, parts of which include those five days in May 1940. At the risk of presumption, I shall venture to say that I have had one advantage over many of them. This has been my knowledge about Hitler — or, rather, my familiarity with documents and other materials relating to him, in this case especially in 1940. For, without understanding what Hitler said and thought and how close he came to winning the war in May 1940, that secondary "duel" between Churchill and Halifax in the War Cabinet seems less important. A flicker of doubt, perhaps; a conflict between two personalities; a footnote in the political history of modern Britain. There were, and are, reasons to look at and treat the five days in London in May 1940 in that way. Such treatments are not necessarily the results of narrowmindedness or excessive specialization. Tightly focused views are often useful, while there is a kind of broadmindedness that can be flat. In this book, however, I have attempted to combine the narrowing acuity of a specialist with a broader perspective, aware that perspective *is* a component of reality itself: in sum, that during those five days in London, the danger, not only to Britain but to the world, was greater and deeper than most people still think.

Acknowledgments

I can recall few books of mine where my debts are as many as they are for this one. Let me list them according to their relative order, though not necessarily according to their relative importance.

I wish to affirm my appreciation for Yale University Press, with which my relations have been untroubled by the problems and irritations that nowadays beset most authors, and especially for the Press's editorial director, Jonathan Brent, and superb manuscript editor Brenda W. Kolb. And to the Earhart Foundation and its secretary, Antony Sullivan, who, as often in the past, were ready and willing and generous in offering financial assistance for my researches in England.

My principal research assistant in the Public Record Office was András D. Bán, whose reliability, precision, and thorough knowledge of the intricacies of the PRO files were invaluable. Joanna Shaw Myers volunteered to accompany me to Cambridge, assisting my passage through the large (and exceptionally well catalogued)

Acknowledgments

Churchill Archives. Among British scholars of modern English history, Philip Bell and Brian Bond gave fine advice and often essential guidance, as did David Astor, David Dilks, M. R. D. Foot, and Andrew Roberts. Among American scholars of British literary history, Samuel Hynes offered the same. The librarian at the Foreign Office in London as well as the archivists and keepers of Churchill College and Trinity College at Cambridge University, of the Neville Chamberlain Papers in the library of the University of Birmingham, of the Halifax diaries and papers in the Borthwick Institute of Historical Research at the University of York, of the Mass-Observation Archives in the University of Sussex of Falmer—Brighton, of the Nicolson diaries in the library of Balliol College at Oxford University, of the Astor papers in the library of the University of Reading, and of the library of King's College in London—all were, without exception, more than benevolent and often especially forthcoming. Edward Baptist, at the University of Pennsylvania, helped in my quest to find books and articles that were not easily available. Helen Hayes, formerly research librarian of Chestnut Hill College, typed a difficult and scribbled-over manuscript under a considerable pressure of time. My wife, Stephanie, reads everything—well, almost everything—that I write; her comments are often funny and incisive, reflections of her sparkling and charming personality, a benison for a manuscript as it is for a man's life.

1997–98

PICKERING CLOSE

(NEAR PHOENIXVILLE, PENNSYLVANIA)

Five Days
in London
May 1940

CHAPTER ONE

The Hinge of Fate

*The turning point. Two accounts. – The awesomeness of the German
tide. – Black Fortnight. – Problems of British morale. –
Distrust of Churchill. – Opinions and sentiments. –
"Outwardly calm, inwardly anxious."*

This book attempts to reconstruct the history of five days that
could have changed the world. The setting is London, and the five
days are Friday through Tuesday, 24 to 28 May 1940. Then and
there Adolf Hitler came closest to winning the Second World War,
his war.

One man who knew how close Hitler had come to his ultimate
victory was Winston Churchill. In the years after the war he gave the
title *The Hinge of Fate* to the fourth volume of his *War Memoirs*. That
volume dealt with the year 1942, near the end of which the Germans
were turned back on many fronts. In November 1942 he said to the
British people that this was not yet the beginning of the end but
perhaps the end of the beginning. November 1942 was the military

hinge of fate on the battlefields of Egypt, North Africa, and Russia: the military turning points. Even then Britain could not win the war. In the end America and Russia did. But in May 1940 Churchill was the one who did not *lose* it. Then and there he saved Britain, and Europe, and Western civilization. And about *that* hinge of fate his *War Memoirs* — essentially his *History of the Second World War* — are largely silent.

In the history of states and of peoples a turning point is often a battle or an episode during a revolution: more precisely, a sudden shifting of events and movements in a battle or during a revolution. A turning point is not a milestone; the latter is a numerically fixable place, foreseeable, linear, and sequential. A turning point may occur in a person's mind; it may mean a change of direction; it has consequences that are multiple and unpredictable, consequences that are more often than not recognizable only in retrospect. A turning point may sometimes be foreseeable, but not with certainty. In this case the moment came late on Tuesday, 28 May. It was the resolution of a struggle which, at that very moment, Churchill had won. He declared that England would go on fighting, no matter what happened. *No matter what happened:* there would be no negotiating with Hitler. Here is his reconstruction of what he said to the Outer Cabinet:

> It was Tuesday, May 28, and I did not attend the House until that day week. There was no advantage to be gained by a further statement in the interval, nor did Members express a wish for one. But everyone realized that the fate of our Army and perhaps much else might well be decided by then. "The House," I said, "should prepare itself for hard and heavy tidings. I have only to add that nothing which may happen in this battle can in any way relieve us of our duty to defend the world

cause to which we have vowed ourselves; nor should it destroy our confidence in our power to make our way, as on former occasions in our history, through disaster and through grief to the ultimate defeat of our enemies." I had not seen many of my colleagues outside the War Cabinet, except individually, since the formation of the Government, and I thought it right to have a meeting in my room at the House of Commons of all the Ministers of Cabinet rank other than the War Cabinet Members. We were perhaps twenty-five round the table. I described the course of events, and I showed them plainly where we were, and all that was in the balance. Then I said quite casually, and not treating it as a point of special significance: "Of course, whatever happens at Dunkirk, we shall fight on."

There occurred a demonstration which, considering the character of the gathering — twenty-five experienced politicians and Parliament men, who represented all the different points of view, whether right or wrong, before the war — surprised me. Quite a number seemed to jump up from the table and came running to my chair, shouting and patting me on the back. There is no doubt that had I at this juncture faltered at all in leading the nation, I should have been hurled out of office. I was sure that every Minister was ready to be killed quite soon, and have all his family and possessions destroyed, rather than give in. In this they represented the House of Commons and almost all the people. It fell to me in these coming days and months to express their sentiments on suitable occasions. This I was able to do, because they were mine also. There was a white glow, overpowering, sublime, which ran through our island from end to end.[1]

1. Churchill, *Their Finest Hour,* 99–100.

This is an inspiring passage — Churchillian, imaginative, descriptive, telling. It is not devoid of truthfulness. There is in it, too, a glimmer of what was perhaps Churchill's finest virtue, his magnanimity: when he suggests that his indomitable resolution to die, if he must, was only a representation of the resolution of others.[2] But what is missing is significant. Here, and indeed in all those long chapters of *Their Finest Hour,* Churchill wrote nothing about the preceding four days, when he had had to struggle to get his way in the War Cabinet. It had been his plan to summon this somewhat extraordinary meeting of the Outer Cabinet, where, as he knew, his supporters were potentially vocal and actually numerous. Moreover, what he said then was *not* said "quite casually, and not treating it as a point of special significance."

There is a fuller description of this meeting in Hugh Dalton's memoirs and his diary. Their substantial tone does not differ much from Churchill's. Dalton was an admirer of Churchill. ("He is quite magnificent. The man, the only man we have, for this hour.") But some of Dalton's details are worth considering. "He was determined," Dalton said of Churchill, "to prepare public opinion for bad tidings, and it would of course be said, and with some truth, that what was now happening in Northern France would be the greatest British military defeat for many centuries." Churchill said, Dalton recalls,

"I have thought carefully in these last days whether it was part of my duty to consider entering negotiations with That Man."[3]

2. "There is no doubt that had I at this juncture faltered at all in leading the nation, I should have been hurled out of office." By whom? By them? And who would succeed him? Was there someone who was more determined to fight Hitler than was Churchill?

3. This first sentence is from Dalton, *The Fateful Years,* 335. The rest coincides with the same diary entry in *The Second World War Diaries of Hugh Dalton,* 27–29.

It was idle to think that, if we tried to make peace now, we should get better terms from Germany than if we went on and fought it out. The Germans would demand our fleet—that would be called "disarmament"—our naval bases, and much else. We should become a slave state, though a British government which would be Hitler's puppet would be set up—"under Mosley or some such person." And where should we be at the end of all that? On the other side, we had immense reserves and advantages. Therefore, he said, "We shall go on and we shall fight it out, here or elsewhere, and if at last the long story is to end, it were better it should end, not through surrender, but only when we are rolling senseless on the ground."[4] There was a murmur of approval round the table, in which I think Amery, Lord Lloyd and I [Dalton] were loudest. Not much more was said. No one expressed even the faintest flicker of dissent. . . . It is quite clear that whereas the Old Umbrella[5]—neither he nor other members of the War Cabinet were at this meeting—wanted to run very early, Winston's bias is all the other way.

Eighteen days before this, on 10 May, Churchill had become prime minister. Late that afternoon, he was driven back from

4. Dalton's marginal insertion: "If this long island story of ours is to end at last, let it end only when each of us lies choking in his own blood upon the ground." (It is possible that, years later, Dalton showed this diary entry to Churchill, who then added or corrected the phrase.)

5. Meaning Chamberlain. Dalton was wrong: the main spokesman for negotiating was Halifax, not Chamberlain. See below, Chapters 2 to 5. Also, the "jumping up, shouting and patting me on the back" episode came at the end of the meeting, not during it. Dalton: "When we separate, several go up and speak to him, and I, patting him on the shoulder, from my physically greater height . . . "

Buckingham Palace to Admiralty House, where he then lived. Behind the driver he sat with Inspector W. H. Thompson, his bodyguard. Churchill was silent. Then Thompson thought it proper to congratulate Churchill. "I only wish the position had come your way in better times for you have an enormous task." Tears came into Churchill's eyes. He said to Thompson: "God alone knows how great it is. I hope it is not too late. I am very much afraid it is. We can only do our best."[6] During the next fourteen days came disaster upon disaster. I am compelled to sum them up at the beginning, after which to the five days in London I shall turn.

♦ ♦ ♦

"I hope it is not too late. I am very much afraid it is." Note that Churchill said this at the moment of his personal triumph, and before the battle in Western Europe began to unfold. But then he had never underestimated Hitler. What even he did not know was that the next fortnight would see Hitler's greatest triumphs: unimaginable, irresistible, perhaps final.

Nearly sixty years after these events, at the end of the twentieth century, the widespread perception is this: Hitler was a fanatic, a dictator, who started a war and turned most of the world against him, a war in which he was bound to fail. There is some truth in this view but not enough. Its shortcoming may be summed up in six words: he was *not* bound to fail. He represented an enormous tide in the affairs of the world in the twentieth century. The force of this tide consisted of the energy, the discipline, the confidence and the obedience, and the vitality of the German people whom he succeeded in uniting beyond the accomplishments of any other leader in their history. He could rely on a national army whose achievements turned out to be awesome, the wonder of the world. More-

---

6. Thompson, *Sixty Minutes with Winston Churchill*, 444.

over — beyond Germany, and in the minds of many people — Hitler's rule, his regime and his ideas, represented a new primary force, beside the corroding alternatives of liberal democracy and "International" Communism. For ten years the tide rose, pounding and pouring over obstacles that disappeared beneath its foaming might. In May 1940 it not only seemed irresistible: in many places and in many ways it was.

Hitler became chancellor of Germany on 30 January 1933. The significance, let alone the importance, of this event went largely unrecognized. Evidence for this exists in the reporting and the commentaries of virtually every leading newspaper of the world.[7] His personal abilities were underestimated, indeed on occasion ridiculed. The German conservative political elite, who helped to arrange his nomination to the chancellorship, thought that they would be able to manage him. The opposite happened. He made them his servitors. More important: soon he became the most popular leader in the history of the Germans, perhaps the most schooled people in the world. The bitterness and the humiliation that had affected most Germans after their loss of the First World War ebbed away; what succeeded it was a rising wave of national self-confidence. To an astonishing degree Hitler won the trust of the great majority of the German people.

For a while his abilities as a statesman went on being unrecog-

7. Churchill recognized Hitler's significance as early as October 1930, two and a half years before Hitler was to become chancellor. Dining at the German embassy in London, the counselor of the embassy, a descendant of Bismarck, considered Churchill's words significant enough to report them to Berlin: "Hitler of course declares he does not intend starting a world war but Churchill believes that Hitler and his followers will grasp the first chance to resort to arms again."

nized. That would change, too, and soon. In three years his Third German Reich replaced France as the leading power in Europe, despite France's multiple alliances, while Hitler did not yet have a single contractual ally. Treaty after treaty restricting Germany militarily, politically, economically, diplomatically, he flung aside. His prestige — and not only among his own people — did not diminish; it rose. Soon the leaders of many European states were seeking his goodwill — or at least they were seeking to avoid any impression that they might be his opponents. Mussolini thought it proper to align himself with this German leader who seemed to be representative of the wave of the future. Less simple were the inclinations of the British governments, of the British Conservative Party, and of many British people. They were inclined to give this new Germany at least the benefit of the doubt. Their policy of appeasing Germany had many motives. We shall have to disentangle some of them later. These inclinations were already apparent during the prime ministership of Stanley Baldwin, but their prototypical representative and proponent was Neville Chamberlain, who became prime minister in 1937. With regard to appeasement his most vocal and determined opponent was Winston Churchill, whose public and political reputation in 1937 stood at what was probably the lowest point in his long career.

It was at that very time that Adolf Hitler chose to plan the imposition of his power beyond the frontiers of Germany, transforming the map of Europe. There were still people who thought he had no talent for statesmanship. Soon they would be dumbfounded or at least numbed. In November 1937 Hitler told his generals that they might as well prepare for war, even though the contingency was not yet immediate, since England, and France dependent on England, had probably written off Austria and Czechoslovakia. This estimate was accurate. A fortnight later it was strengthened when Chamberlain (unaware, of course, of what Hitler was planning) chose his confidant Lord Halifax to travel to Germany on a goodwill visit, very much including a meeting with Hitler. Halifax was, as was his wont, cautious (in this case, cautious rather than circumspect), but he did suggest to Hitler that the British government would not oppose Germany as long as Germany would achieve its ambitions without war. In February 1938 Anthony Eden resigned as Chamberlain's foreign secretary; his place was taken by Halifax. Churchill recorded in his *War Memoirs* that he instantly recognized the portent of this change: he, a champion sleeper, now spent a largely sleepless night.[8]

1938 was Hitler's year. In March he occupied and annexed Austria without firing a single shot, indeed accompanied by the enthusiasm of the mass of the Austrian people. Immediately he turned on Czechoslovakia, which he succeeded in breaking up, adding a large portion of it, with millions of German-speaking people, to his Greater German Reich and reducing the rest to a near-satellite status. This despite the fact that, unlike Austria, Czechoslovakia had military alliances: with Soviet Russia and, more important, with France, behind which Britain seemed to stand. Seemed to stand: for that was the crux of the matter. France would not go to war except together with Britain, and Britain was not willing to do so. The main reason for this was British unpreparedness — militarily, to be sure; but beyond and beneath such practical calculations there was the unpreparedness of the people, of British opinion, and of the leaders of the Dominions for another European war for the sake of Czechoslovakia. Even that was not all. There was the reasoning of Chamberlain, not merely to delay but to avoid a confrontation with

8. About another momentous and sleepless night in the life of Lord Halifax in 1938, see pp. 64–65.

Hitler, to whom he was inclined to give the benefit of the doubt, even in extreme situations. Hence the last-minute conference at Munich when Czechoslovakia was surrendered and when Chamberlain was not only relieved but, at least temporarily, encouraged by the prospect of an Anglo-German understanding which could mean Peace In Our Time. Churchill attacked Chamberlain, but to no avail. In a great speech in the House of Commons, Churchill declared that this was all wrong, that "we have sustained a total and unmitigated defeat." His speech was telling and prophetic, but only in retrospect. Except among a small and anxious minority, Churchill's reputation and his influence were still at a low ebb; he was nearly censured by his own constituency. To this we may add that in one important respect Churchill was wrong. It would have been disastrous for the Western democracies to go to war in October 1938.[9] He may have been right, morally speaking; practically, he was wrong.

Hitler, at the same time, appeared as the greatest leader and statesman that the German people had had in one thousand years — as well as the most powerful national leader in Europe, perhaps even in the world. But he was not made in the classic stamp of a statesman. He was relentless, pressed by a deep sense that time was working against him. He was not content to digest his conquests and to solidify his triumphs. In March 1939 he made a grave mistake. He marched into Prague, incorporating the broken remnant of Czechoslovakia into his Greater German Empire. Thereby he broke his word of six months before ("my last territorial demand," and so on) as well as the asseveration of his main purpose, that of the uniting in

---

9. He was wrong, too, in his conviction that in 1938 Stalin's Russia would have gone to war on the side of the Czechs. He wrote this as late as 1948, in volume 1 of his *Second World War.* Yet Stalin was even less inclined to honor his military pact with the Czechs than were the French.

one Reich all German peoples, to the exclusion of non-German ones, along the principle of national self-determination (a principle that, alas, had been proclaimed and espoused by Woodrow Wilson). The result was a belated, but instant, revolution of British opinion. Chamberlain's first inclination was to accept the inevitable, that is, Hitler's occupation of Czechoslovakia, the end result of a process that, after all, had been foreordained in Munich. But the pressure of public opinion and the press was now too much. Even Chamberlain's foreign secretary, Halifax, was no longer in favor of appeasing Hitler. Halifax's influence contributed considerably to Chamberlain's speech at Birmingham, three days after Hitler's arrival in Prague. It was in effect a declaration of the British government: "thus far and no further." One week after Prague Hitler took another sliver of former German territory from Lithuania, and the German propaganda apparatus started a campaign against Poland. Now the British government advanced a guarantee to Poland, with the aim of deterring Hitler. It did not work; but, in any event, even Chamberlain was now compelled to envision the prospect of a war. And now Churchill's reputation started to rise. He did not have the habit of saying "I told you so," but about Hitler he seemed to have been proved right. During the summer of 1939 Chamberlain was still inclined to find some kind of an accommodation with Hitler. But the constraints and conditions were too strenuous for that. On the day that Hitler invaded Poland, Chamberlain invited Churchill into his cabinet, as the first lord of the Admiralty. Until the last moment Chamberlain was reluctant to declare war on Germany. But by 3 September he had no choice.

Hitler hoped that this would not happen. In this he was wrong. But he was not wrong in knowing that Chamberlain and the British went to war reluctantly — indeed, that apart from their declarations of war, the British and the French would do little or nothing, except perhaps on the seas. The still-accepted idea that while the German armies were fighting in Poland an Allied ground offensive across the so-called Siegfried Line would not only have been possible but deci-- sive is groundless: it was not possible because it was not planned, and it was not planned because it was not possible. The result was eight months of what American journalists dubbed the Phoney War (Reluctant War may have been a better term). During it Churchill's popularity grew, to the extent that many people were inclined to overlook his mistakes. All this came to a head when Hitler invaded Denmark and Norway in early April 1940 — perhaps his most daring move of the entire war. The British response was miserable. The navy missed the Germans; it was unable to prevent German land-ings along the long coast of Norway; where British troops were landed, here and there, they soon retreated rather abjectly; they were outmarched and outfought by the Germans nearly everywhere. Churchill was responsible for much of this. It was his attempt to establish a British presence along the Norwegian coast that made Hitler decide to invade that country; and Churchill's directives to the British fleet were often wrongheaded.

Still, the defeat in Norway brought down the Chamberlain gov-ernment. There arose in the House of Commons a heated and con-fused debate propelled by the rising sentiment that Chamberlain was not the right person to lead Britain through the war. There was a sig-nificant vote when dozens of his own Conservative Party members deserted him. Churchill stood by him, unreservedly loyal, though knowing that his own hour might have come. On 9 May Cham-berlain concluded that he had to resign. There must be a National Government, including ministers from the Labour Party. His pre-ferred successor was Halifax. Most of the Conservatives preferred Halifax. The king preferred Halifax. There was still plenty of distrust, (even though momentarily latent) of Churchill. But Halifax demurred. There perhaps were three reasons for this. He was a member of the House of Lords, which presented a constitutional problem, though one that could have been fixed. He may or may not have been acceptable to Labour, though that too was not certain. What decided the matter for him was his own judgment that within a Halifax cabinet Churchill the warrior would be unmanageable. Late in the afternoon of 10 May Churchill went to Buckingham Palace, and returned as prime minister.

Eight years later he wrote that he was "conscious of a profound sense of relief": "At last I had the authority to give directions over the whole scene."[10] But: had he not said to Inspector Thompson, "I hope it is not too late"? Behind the horseman sat black care.

With every reason. There was a fateful coincidence on that historic day. "Coincidences are spiritual puns" (Chesterton). On 10 May 1940 the pun was more than spiritual. Early that morning the German invasion of Western Europe began. Hitler, who had not only planned it but chosen its main design — again he would be underestimated, this time as a strategist and military leader — was at his headquarters, near the German-Belgian border, watching the campaign develop. This thunderclap on 10 May had nothing to do with Churchill's ascent to the prime ministership; that had been virtually decided the day before. Nor do we have any evidence that, when the news of Churchill's appointment reached Hitler at the end of the day, he was affected by it. He had a contempt for Churchill because of Churchill's insistent opposition to him and because of what he knew about Churchill's character and personal habits; he underestimated Churchill — wrongly, as things turned out, though that would not be

10. Churchill, *Their Finest Hour,* 667.

apparent until many months later. He thought that Churchill would not last long, that Churchill's belligerent manner and his warlike instincts were not shared by most people of the British establishment.

Again Hitler was not altogether wrong. When Churchill appeared in the House of Commons three days after his appointment, he was greeted with little or no enthusiasm by the Conservative Party, many members of which now seemed to have been in a mild state of emotional hangover, slightly ashamed of the burst of emotion that had helped to bring Chamberlain down. Lord Davidson wrote to Stanley Baldwin: "The Tories don't trust Winston. . . . After the first clash of war is over it may well be that a sounder Government may emerge."[11] Churchill knew how dependent he was on the Conservative Party, and on Chamberlain. He treated the latter with a compound of prudence and magnanimity. ("I am in your hands," he wrote to Chamberlain.) He brought a few new people into his cabinet, but the composition of it did not change drastically. All of this is known by historians, and we shall return to evidences of a distrust for Churchill. When on 13 May he made his famous "blood, sweat, toil and tears" speech, so impressive when read now, and emotionally honest, it was not too well received by many Conservatives in the House.

But it was the greater and dramatic and terrifying flow of events that we must now consider: the fact that the first fortnight of Churchill's prime ministership was a time of crashing disasters. Disasters for Britain and Churchill, triumphs for Germany and Hitler. Here was the proof of a new model German army, welded together by an

11. Cited in Gilbert, *Finest Hour,* 327. Colville Diary (Churchill Archives, referred to as CA, below), 11 May: "There seems to be some inclination in Whitehall to believe that Winston will be a complete failure and that Neville will return."

iron sense of national self-confidence, directed by a new model of generalship, equipped with new visions and new armor for a new kind of warfare. Three days after their start the Germans broke across the French lines at Sedan. Holland surrendered. Brussels was abandoned. On the tenth day the Germans were at the English Channel, which they had not been able to reach during the entire First World War. The French and British armies in Flanders and Belgium were trapped. In many places the French fought not at all. Churchill flew over the Channel to Paris twice, encouraging their leaders, but with not much effect. Some of their military chiefs and politicians were beginning to consider the necessity for an armistice with the Germans, through the mediation of Mussolini. Mussolini all but declared that Italy would soon enter the war on Hitler's side. The plan for a French-British counterattack, aimed at cutting through the nose of the advancing German armored crocodile,[12] did not come about. The British, and Churchill, were now forced to begin considering the removal of the British Expeditionary Force across the Channel — if that were possible at all. British and French troops were pushed back to Boulogne and Calais, presently surrounded by the Germans. And if the French fought badly or not at all, the British in Belgium fought not much better (except, perhaps, in the air, but there, too, their attempts at bombing important bridges were useless). On the ground, except for one failed countermove at Arras, the BEF had engaged in no real battles with the Germans; its falling back was more orderly than that of the French, but still it was retreat after retreat.

The Germans seemed invincible, and the world was stunned. So was Hitler. He hardly believed his luck. For once, he was more cau-

12. On 15 May, to the Chiefs of Staff Committee, Churchill spoke of "this battle of the Bulge."

tious than were many of his generals. For once, his self-confidence —
his greatest asset, which, throughout his career, rested on his feral,
instinctive understanding of his opponents' weaknesses — wobbled
a bit. He was nervous and worried. He did not quite realize what his
German troops were capable of. During the days of his army's
most rapid advances — the seventeenth and the eighteenth — he kept
warning his generals against the dangers of a British-French counterattack, which never came. There was another, probably more
important matter on his mind. He thought that the British would
soon recognize the futility of warring against him. He believed that
Churchill's days as leader were numbered, that the British would
soon turn away from Churchill and respond to a peace offer from
him. On 21 May he told General Franz Halder, "We are seeking
contact with England on the basis of a division of the world." The
English would see the light, sooner rather than later. He, Hitler, was
astride a great wave, representing the Present and perhaps the Future. Churchill was struggling on the shore, representing an antiquated and useless Past. Hitler also thought that he had the trust and
faith of the vast majority of Germans, more than Churchill could
count on among the British. Was he altogether wrong? Yes and no.
No, because this was how things *seemed,* and while what happens
may not be identical with what people think happens in the long
run, the two are inseparable in the short run. Yes, because the majority of the British people refused to recognize how close Hitler had
come to an ultimate triumph and how close they had come to their
ultimate defeat. But their martial spirit was not unwavering, and
they were not — yet — annealed to Churchill.

◆ ◆ ◆

In a secret memorandum to the War Cabinet, Robert Boothby
(a Conservative MP and a Churchillian) wrote on 20 March that
Hitler's Germans represented "the incredible conception of a *move-*

ment — young, virile, dynamic, and violent — which is advancing irresistibly to overthrow a decaying old world, that we must continually bear in mind; for it is the main source of the Nazi strength and power."[13] On the very day that the real war broke out in the West, Chamberlain wrote in his diary that Joseph Kennedy (the defeatist American ambassador) told him that he didn't see how Britain could carry on without the French: "I told him I did not see how we could either."[14] On 15 May Lieutenant General Henry Pownall wrote in his diary, sizing up what had happened to the French at the Meuse and Sedan. "Three armies to withdraw because of the initiative shown by one German battalion commander."[15] On 17 May the Ministry of Information suggested to the War Cabinet that "more should be done to inform the general public of the seriousness of the situation, about which most people [are] in complete ignorance."[16] Most people, perhaps, but not all of them. On 14–15 May a quarter of a million queued up at the local police stations to enroll in the Local Defense Volunteers, soon to be renamed the Home Guard. But on 17 May the society photographer Cecil Beaton, on his way to America, wrote in his diary, "My own private

13. CA, 20–21. On 19 June Boothby returned to the same argument in a letter to Churchill.

14. Chamberlain Diary, 10 May, NC 2/24 A.

15. Pownall, *Chief of Staff,* with an excellent introduction by Bond. General Pownall was very intelligent but not always a good judge of men. In 1939 he praised the French general Huntziger: "a very good head on his shoulders" (214). Huntziger was responsible, among other things, for the neglect of the French defense preparation at the Ardennes and the Meuse. About Leslie Hore-Belisha, the minister of war 1938–39, he wrote, "an obscure shallow-brained, charlatan, political jewboy" (203). About Churchill, in 1936: "Churchill of course is hopeless."

16. War Cabinet 65/7, 17 May.

courage was badly bruised, and each person one spoke to was more depressing than the last. . . . A mood of panic was gripping upper-class circles."[17] General Sir Edmund Ironside, chief of the Imperial General Staff, wrote in his diary on the same day, "At the moment it looks like the greatest military disaster in all history."[18]

On the eighteenth, Sir Samuel Hoare wrote in his diary: "Neville completely knocked out. Everything finished. The USA no good. We could never get our army out, nor if we did it would be without any equipment."[19] (This even before the Germans reached the Channel.)

That very day, Churchill, at the end of a dispatch to General Ismay, for the first time raised the possibility of a French surrender: "The Chiefs of Staff must consider whether it would not be well to send only half the so-called Armoured Division to France. One must always be prepared for the fact that the French may be offered very advantageous terms of peace, and the whole weight be thrown on us."[20] On 19 May, returning from the cabinet and walking "the ugly staircase of the War Office to [his] room, General Ironside told Anthony Eden: 'This is the end of the British Empire.' He spoke the words flatly and as a mere statement of military fact. He did not believe that we could hold out alone for more than a few months."[21]

17. Cited in Calder, *The People's War,* 106.

18. *Ironside Diaries,* 316–17. The same Ironside earlier, in March: the Germans were poor, "their attack in the West would be a terrible gamble for them" (241).

19. Hoare Diary, 18 May, XII/2, cited in a superb doctoral dissertation: Esnouf, "British Government War Aims and Attitudes," 189.

20. CA, 20/13.

21. Eden, *The Reckoning,* 107. (But also: "One day at the War Cabinet when the news had been more than usually discouraging, the P.M. looked at me across the table and remarked: 'About time that No. 17 turned up, isn't it?'" No. 17 was Churchill's favorite marker, his winning chip at the roulette tables in Monte Carlo and Cannes.)

On 19 May Oliver Harvey wrote in his diary, "Defeatism in London among the richer classes."[22] On the same day Chamberlain in his diary: "The scene . . . darken[s] every hour." A day later: "Nothing to relieve anxiety." On the twenty-first: the situation is "desperate." On the twenty-third: "another bleak day." The French "had done nothing," their generals were "beneath contempt," and their soldiers, "with some exceptions, . . . would not fight and not even march."[23]

At night on the twenty-first, Churchill's new secretary, John Colville: "Dined at Betty Montagu's flat . . . and tried unsuccessfully not to talk about the war. . . . It is clear that the full horror of the situation is dawning on people."[24] On 22 May Charles Waterhouse, a Conservative MP, no friend of Churchill's, wrote in his diary, " 'All is lost' sort of attitude in evidence in many quarters."[25]

"Many quarters" may be too vague and — perhaps — exaggerated. "All is lost": *that* kind of defeatism was not discernible, at least not among the mass of the people. Note, too, that these were the days (the twenty-first to the twenty-fourth, Tuesday to Friday) when both the press and the government expected the French-British counteroffensive at Arras-Amiens against the Bulge (an expectation also propelled by false news); when there came the news of the change of the French high command, the sacking of General Maurice Gamelin and his replacement by General Maxime Weygand, from whom much was expected; when Boulogne, Calais, and

22. Esnouf, "British Government War Aims and Attitudes," 90.

23. Chamberlain Diary, NC 1/20, cited also in Lawlor, *Churchill and the Politics of War,* 54–55.

24. Colville Diary, 21 May: "But I think Betts was typical of the whole country when she said 'we shall not be beaten, even if Paris and London fall we shall win.'" As late as 23 May Colville still misspelled "Dunkirque."

25. In Roberts, *Eminent Churchillians,* 159.

Dunkirk were still in Allied hands, indeed the first two filled by units shipped to them from England. Yet cracks were appearing in morale, and the incompetence of the War Office was becoming fatefully evident. The Germans began their siege of Boulogne on the twenty-second. The arms ordered by the War Office, shipped mostly in the large vessel *City of Christchurch,* were badly packed and often unusable. "At 9 P.M. the ship's crew and the stevedores refused to continue [the unloading] owing to the visit of the Luftwaffe." An officer "even had to place some of the crew under guard."[26] Meanwhile, two elite British units, the First Battallion of the Queen Victoria Rifles and the Rifle Brigade (the Green Jackets), were shipped to Calais on the twenty-second and twenty-third, put under the command of Brigadier Claude Nicholson, a brave officer who was to die in German captivity. As Airey Neave (a Churchillian) wrote: "Whatever may be said of the ultimate merit of Churchill's decision to hold Calais 'to the death,' the manner in which [these regiments] were hastily dispatched to France was shameful. . . . [In their story] farce and tragedy are intimately combined. . . . Their orders were depressingly obscure and they had no idea what to expect on arrival at Calais." There, too, on 23 May, stevedores refused to work when the German shells began to fall; a Rifle Brigade officer had to find and force them out from "various holes and corners."[27]

During these crucial days the conduct of the command in London, that is, the management of the war by the War Office, beggars belief, marked as it was by lassitude, incompetence, and confusion.

◆ ◆ ◆

During these days Churchill's position was not — yet — shaken. Perhaps the habitual slowness of British minds contributed to that;

26. Neave, *The Flames of Calais,* 50.
27. Ibid., 56, 85.

perhaps—and this is more likely—there seemed to be as yet no alternative to him, no spokesman for a course other than his. Still, the record of his past—his mistakes, the oddity of his character— was a burden, even though he did not see it that way. Nonetheless we must sum up some of its ingredients, together with some of the evidences of the distrust with which many of his own party saw him during these rapidly darkening days and nights.

"Although he was an aristocrat by birth, Churchill was widely believed to be not really a gentleman at all. On the contrary, he was often described as a highly gifted, but undeniable, 'cad.'" He was "widely distrusted as a man of unstable temperament, unsound judgment, and rhetorical (and also alcoholic) excess. . . . For most of his career, there hung around him an unsavoury air of disreputability and unseemliness, as a particularly wayward, rootless and anachronistic product of a decaying and increasingly discredited aristocratic order. Before 1940, it was not easy for him to be taken seriously as the man of destiny he believed himself to be, when so many people in the know regarded him as little better than an ungentlemanly, almost déclassé, adventurer." During the interwar years he remained "a shameless cadger and incorrigible scrounger." "[His] friends were almost invariably drawn from [a] raffish world." "By the mid-1930s . . . [he] had become almost a parody of the paranoid aristocrat: intransigent, embittered, apocalyptic, 'a reactionary of the deepest dye.'"[28] These generalizations by David Cannadine have the mark of a heavy pen; they are somewhat exaggerated, but they are not without substance. Perhaps more balanced, but not essentially different, are the summary sentences by Andrew Roberts. "The national saviour

28. Cannadine, *Aspects of Aristocracy,* 132, 147, 159, 161. Nancy Astor to Stewart Perowne, 8 January 1940: "I still don't want him as Prime Minister" (Astor Papers, 2/206, 1416).

image of Winston Churchill in 1940 is so deeply ingrained into the British psyche as to make any criticism of his conduct during that year sound almost blasphemous. At the outset of that annus mirabilis, however, he was not considered the splendid personification of British glory he was to become later on. Rather he was seen by many in society and in the Conservative Party as a political turncoat, a dangerous adventurer." At best he was a "delightful rogue who lacked political judgment," at worst "unscrupulous, unreliable, and unattractively ambitious." Churchill's wit and oratorical ability were not enough to overcome severe doubts about his judgment."[29] Besides, some of his enemies often referred to him as a "half-breed" (his mother having been American, and a woman with more than one past) or a "mongrel."

Much of this would change in 1940. But not immediately. It is of course not our task here to describe or analyze the ups and downs in the long history of Winston Churchill's reputation. But we must be concerned with him during the fateful fortnight of 10 to 24 May. On 10 May the king evidently preferred Halifax, with whom he and the queen (who disliked Churchill) had had very good private relations. (They had dined together on occasion; Halifax also had the key to the palace garden.) There was, too, an "almost universal expectation that Churchill's ministry was going to be short-lived."[30] "Almost universal" may be too much, but, again, it was not without serious substance. Many, perhaps most, of the Conservative MPs distrusted Churchill. They cheered Chamberlain and sat on their hands when Churchill first appeared in the House of Commons as prime minister. Churchill noticed and remembered this (David Lloyd George thought that Churchill was afraid of Chamberlain). During the

29. Roberts, *The Holy Fox,* 187–88.
30. Ibid., 203.

Black Fortnight these opponents of Churchill had few reasons to change their minds. Now the talkative warmonger had his chance. And what had he brought about, as so often in his mercurial past? Nothing but disaster after disaster — in spite of the artifice of his rhetoric, in spite of his habitual declarations, and not only in spite of but because of his habitual trust in the French.

The words "crooks," "gangsters," and "wild men" appear in many of the diaries and letters of the period, referring to Churchill's new government. Among the papers of reputable members of the establishment and the government, those of Lord Hankey, who was still chancellor of the duchy of Lancaster, are illustrative.[31] On 10 May Hankey wrote to his son: "The net result of it all is that today, when the greatest battle of the war and probably the greatest battle of our history has begun, when the fate of the whole Empire is at stake, we are to have a Government of politicians, . . . quite a number of whom are perfectly futile people." To Samuel Hoare two days later: "God help the country . . . which commits its existence to the hands of a dictator whose past achievements, even though inspired by a certain amount of imagination, have never achieved success! . . . An untried and wholly inexperienced politician. . . . The only hope lies in the solid core of Churchill, Chamberlain and Halifax, but whether the wise old elephants will ever be able to hold the Rogue Elephant, I doubt." Hoare answered on 14 May: "Are you and I partners in adversity? I do not know!" Chamberlain, who (unlike Halifax) refrained from criticizing Churchill, was critical of Churchill's "method of government making," though only in his diary and in his letters to his sister. Among the military chiefs, Lieutenant General Henry Pownall made scathing comments in his diary. On 30 April, before the change of government, he charged: "Great as are

31. His letters in CA; in his diary the years 1938–44 are largely weeded out.

[Churchill's] uses he is also a real danger, always tempted by the objective, never counting his resources to see if the objective is attainable. And he is *unlucky*. He was throughout the last war; and that is a real thing and a bad and dangerous failing." On 20 May, about a move toward Amiens: "a scandalous (i.e. Winstonized) plan." On 24 May: "Here are Winston's plans again. Can nobody prevent his trying to conduct operations himself as a super Commander-in-Chief? How does he think we are to collect eight divisions and attack as he suggests. He can have no conception of our situation and conditions. How is an attack like this to be staged involving three nationalities at an hour's notice? [This was an unfair analysis of the then situation.] The man is mad."[32]

Yet those who were now working close to Churchill began to appreciate some of his qualities. A telling example is John Colville's diary entries, for two reasons. One is the gradual and apparently genuine conversion of a young upper-class person and civil servant from a distrust of to a respect for Churchill; the other is that the Colville diary (including his fine handwriting) is a period piece, surely of May 1940. On 9 May: "Wagered . . . a champagne dinner that Mr. C. [Chamberlain] would still be Prime Minister by the end of the month. . . . Dined with Mrs Henley and went on afterwards to dance at the Savoy. . . . I thought . . . the Churchill girl [Mary] rather supercilious. . . . The Savoy was stuffy and I felt jaded, devitalized and utterly uninteresting." Next morning (a radiant morning, and Hitler's D-Day): "Rode at Richmond in summer heat. As I dismounted the groom told me that Holland and Belgium had been invaded. Nothing can stop [Churchill] having his way—because of his powers of blackmail. . . . Rab [R. A. Butler, who hated Churchill] said that the good clean tradition of English politics, that of

32. Pownall, *Chief of Staff,* 304, 323, 333.

Pitt opposed to Fox, had been sold to the greatest adventurer of modern political history . . . this sudden coup of Winston and his rabble . . . "[33] On 13 May: "Went down to the House to hear the new Prime Minister. . . . He made a brilliant little [little?] speech." But also: "I spent the day in a bright blue suit from the Fifty-Shilling Tailors, cheap and sensational-looking, which I felt was appropriate to the new Government." Three days later some respect for Churchill is already discernible in Colville's diary, though, deciphering Churchill's telegram to the Cabinet from Paris (including phrases such as "the mortal gravity of the hour"), Colville still records the remarks of two other secretaries: "He is still thinking of his books" and "his blasted rhetoric." And by 18 May a certain admiration appears: "Winston, who is full of fight and thrives on crisis and adversity . . . " Colville has also begun to have an appreciation of Churchill's carefulness: "Such is the change that high office can work in a man's inherent love of rash and spectacular action."[34]

On 19 May Churchill first broadcast to the people through the

33. Much later, in his diaries, Colville pasted a newspaper clipping of a speech by Butler in London in May 1943: "An immortal Prime Minister. Never since the time of Chatham had Britain occupied so prominent a position in the countries of the world nor had any Prime Minister led the armies and navies and air forces of the world towards saving civilization as Mr. Churchill was now doing."

34. Colville Diary, CA. Butler's willingness to keep intriguing against Churchill is also evident from the letters he wrote to Colville at the time. On 17 May: "I am really very sorry that you are no longer one of the team [that is, the Chamberlain team] and that you have been sacrificed for the Coalition. *Do* let me know what you are doing, so that we can meet. I hope we shall keep in touch for the sake of the future, the need for more intimate contact is what we have all learned from recent experiences" (Butler Papers, G 11 74, G 11 75).

BBC. It was a good speech, but it included a fateful sentence: "For myself, I have invincible confidence in the French army and its leaders." This was not true. His confidence in the French army, far from being "invincible," was in fact running out. He had already begun to contemplate that the French might give up fighting altogether. During the next seven days he tried to pursue two parallel courses of action which, in the end, proved contradictory. One was essentially continental, the other essentially maritime. One was to urge a French-British counteroffensive aimed at the German Bulge, or Snout, the other to prepare the withdrawal of the entire British army from the Continent. One meant sending yet more troops to Boulogne and Calais, but only for the other purpose, to slow down the German advance toward the last evacuation port of Dunkirk. Churchill flew over to Paris again and seems to have returned in good spirits. But late in the morning of the twenty-third, Monday, he told the War Cabinet: "The whole success of the plan agreed with the French depended on the French forces taking the offensive. At present they showed no signs of doing that. . . . If General Weygand's plan succeeded" — and we know now that Weygand never had such a plan[35] — "it would mean the release of 35 Allied divisions from their present serious predicament. If it failed, it would be necessary to make a fresh plan with the object of saving and bringing back to this country as many of our best troops and weapons with as little loss as possible."[36] *With as little loss as possible.* Churchill knew that that was almost impossible. His household diary records that he then returned to his quarters in Admiralty House for lunch and that dinner on 23 May was short. Later, after dinner, he went to Buck-

35. On 22 May Weygand telephoned Ironside, saying that the French had recaptured Amiens, Albert, and Péronne. This was untrue.

36. CAB 65 / 7, 23 May.

ingham Palace to see the king. At half past ten he told the king that if the French plan failed, he would have to order the BEF back to England. "This operation would mean the loss of all guns, tanks, ammunition, and all stores in France," the king recorded in his diary. "The question was whether we could get the troops back from Calais and Dunkirk. The very thought of having to order this movement is appalling, *as the loss of life will probably be immense.*"[37]

♦ ♦ ♦

Such was the situation when night fell on Thursday, 23 May 1940. At least one-quarter of a million British troops were trapped by the Germans. They were retreating rather than making a stand, still not putting up much fight against the probing advance of their enemies. Boulogne had fallen, and Calais was beginning to be surrounded by the Germans. Meanwhile, General Heinz Wilhelm Guderian was approaching Dunkirk from the south; other German generals were leaning against the retreating BEF from the east. There were not many British troops left to the south, in the rest of France, and not much of an army in Britain itself.

The British people knew some of this but not much. The tone of the BBC was well mannered and somber, not providing misleading or inaccurate news, but also not suggesting what the Germans' surrounding of the quarter million meant. The newspapers' reporting was generally inaccurate: they gave the impression of a great historic battle in northern France, with little indication of what the portents might be. But in May 1940 the radio and the press did not quite reflect or form what the British people were thinking. And we must turn to other sources and attempt to reconstruct something of the thinking and the mood of the people, no matter how incomplete

37. From the diary of King George VI, John Wheeler-Bennett, *King George VI*.

Churchill crossing Horse Guards Parade on 20 May: "On 19 May Churchill first broadcast to the people through the BBC. It was a good speech, but it included a fateful sentence: 'For myself, I have invincible confidence in the French army and its leaders.' This was not true . . . "

such a reconstruction must necessarily be. The reason for this is that by 1940 the world, or at least the Western world, had entered the democratic age. "Opinion," Pascal had written three hundred years before, "is the queen of the world." But unlike three hundred years earlier, now the opinion (or, more precisely, the thinking) of majorities mattered. Hitler knew this. He knew that he had the overwhelming majority of the German people behind him. What mattered was whether the great majority of the British people were really behind Churchill. And, if so, for how long?

Before we attempt this necessarily incomplete sketch of this important matter, we must keep two conditions in mind. One is the seldom recognized difference between public opinion and popular sentiment. Briefly put: that which is public is not necessarily popular, and opinion is not necessarily the same thing as sentiment. There are many examples in history, and not the least in the history of democracies, when public opinion and popular sentiment are not only different but often diverge.[38] In the nineteenth century, public opinion was the opinion of the middle and upper classes, not of the lower, or working, class, even though working-class people gradually became newspaper readers and voters. Much of this class distinction was still evident in Britain in 1940, although fortuitously it proved not to be decisive. But it did exist, and we have now seen

---

38. It is interesting that Churchill, at least in one instance, impatiently confused the two. On 5 February 1940, he told the newspaper proprietor Cecil King, "This time of war the machinery of government was so strong that it could largely afford to ignore popular feeling." More bluntly, he thought that Prime Minister Chamberlain "could afford to say: 'to hell with public opinion'" (Bell, "British Public Opinion on the War," 38, citing Cecil H. King, *With Malice Toward None,* 22). Bell adds, "[And yet] it was eventually public opinion expressed through the press and the House of Commons, which brought down Chamberlain's government"—and brought Churchill to power (ibid.).

some of its evidences — for example, the "panic" that seemed to have gripped some people in the upper classes on 18–19 May. Yet nothing of that had filtered down into the newspapers, and the great majority of people were unaware of it. What it signifies is that, here and there, *some* people (mostly in London) became suddenly aware of the seeming hopelessness of the situation.

Another group of people among whom evidences of defeatism existed in mid-May were intellectuals. "The artist," Ezra Pound once wrote, "is the antennae of the race." But in 1940 this was not so. Cyril Connolly, not a defeatist (he started his *Horizon* in January 1940), feared that in the event of German bombing the people would panic (George Orwell told him that he did not agree). In the surviving writings and reminiscences of writers the record about May 1940 is confusing and mixed. In *Put Out More Flags* (written in 1942), Evelyn Waugh wrote of "that odd, dead period before the Churchillian renaissance." (The book ends in June 1940: "There's a new spirit abroad. . . . I see it on every side.")[39] Ten years later, in *Men at Arms,* there is not one glimmer of a Churchillian renaissance; indeed, Waugh said that he abhorred Churchill and his rhetoric, as did Malcolm Muggeridge (but he, too, only well after the war). There is no Churchillian renaissance, indeed, nothing of May 1940, in Anthony Powell's *Valley of Bones,* the seventh novel in his *Dance to the Music of Time,* which is set during the first half of 1940. Careful readers may detect a suggestive element in Kenneth Clark's autobiographical *Another Part of the Wood: A Self-Portrait* (1974). Clark

---

39. Waugh had joined the army and kept a diary. On 19 May there is an admiring and funny note about Churchill. On 20 May: "Returned to camp to find bad news of the war." On 22 May: "I lectured the company about the international situation and depressed myself so much that I could barely continue speaking" (*Diaries,* 469).

was not a typical intellectual but, rather, a knowledgeable and well-situated figure within the upper reaches of the establishment. Elegant and sleek, he was for years rather close to Chamberlain. In these memoirs, decades after the war, he writes sympathetically but critically of Chamberlain: "I was in fact unequivocally on the side of Mr. Churchill.[40] Unequivocally? Not — yet — in May 1940.

The other distinction that we must keep in mind is the one between understanding and knowing. To invoke Pascal again: "We understand more than we know." According to logic, understanding is not only the result of knowledge; it necessarily follows knowledge. Yet there are myriad instances and examples when understanding precedes knowledge, indeed, when it *leads* to knowledge. Allow me, then, to essay this generalization: in May 1940 most British men and women *understood* some things that they did not yet *know.* Or they understood some things that they did not wish to think about, even as they were capable of thinking about them (a very British inclination). We shall, I hope, give some illustrations of this in the following pages, indeed, throughout this book.[41]

There exist numerous books and diaries and reminiscences of people and writers about the late summer of 1940 and the Blitz, but

40. Clark, *Another Part of the Wood,* 268. Though about Churchill, "When he writes in a Gibbonian manner, I do not admire his prose" (273).

41. "It was very difficult to sound as if we were unbearably chilly and matter-of-fact, like English people in foreign plays, but the danger was so *close,* the appalling size of the smash-up so apparent, that the only thing to do was what everyone else was doing, keeping a steady eyes-front. Once you looked sideways, once you looked round, once you let your imagination out, you knew you might lose your head. Clearly the thing to do was to get yourself into a certain definite frame of mind and keep it at all costs, even if it made you slightly stupid. Everyone I met in the village seemed to be doing this instinctively" (Allingham, *The Oaken Heart,* 170).

not very many about May 1940. One exception is *The Oaken Heart,* by the detective-story writer Margery Allingham. The book is a kind of diary, reproduced (and perhaps edited here and there) for her American friends, about "Auburn," the village in Essex where she lived. Since a fair amount of it was written during the Black Fortnight in May 1940, it may be worth citing parts of it here in some detail.[42] On 14 or 15 May Allingham heard Queen Wilhelmina speaking on the BBC: "Showed us country people that she was a proper Queen, . . . [but] she brought something else right home to many of us. *Courage was not going to be enough.* For the first time probably in all our history we were not going to get by, this time, with just courage and the improvisation it brings with it." On Sunday morning (most probably 19 May), Allingham talks with a former corporal of the First World War: "That was the first time I ever heard anyone in the country question the reliability of the French, although some informed circles [in London] had been whispering about it uneasily for months. Mr Parker said he only hoped that there was some sort of a trap waiting somewhere, and that in the past we had permitted dangerous advances for that very purpose." On 20 May: "The method of the German advance fascinated everybody. In the next few days it was discussed exhaustively by everyone who came in and who we met in the square." Also: "The Captain

42. "The actual day-to-day history of these two months, April and May 1940, is now known to everybody who can read. . . . It makes a savage but coherent tale, one thing following ruthlessly and logically upon the next, but at the time in Auburn (who like the child in the crowd at the barrier, not seeing any better for being in the front row) nothing seemed at all logical. We got to hear of things in a slightly different order from the true one. Some of them, the evacuation of Dunkirk, for instance, we got wind of before many other people, but others, like the shakiness of France, we realized long after most" (ibid., 154).

admired the enemy efficiency from a purely professional point of view. You had to hand it to that feller Hitler, he said, He knew how to get a move on."[43] Unlike during the First World War, there was now the prospect of invasion.

The next morning we were still not invaded. Still no German soldiers, with or without disguise, had dropped out of the sky, and I could not help hoping with Norry, who insisted "all this will pass," as if it were a stone or a tree, that it would never come. However, we knew it was criminal just to hope. Already the cry "wishful thinking" was being thrown at us bitterly as if we had originated the sin and we were inclined to resent it. (There is a tendency to take everything very personally in Auburn.) We had never been optimists about anything and had been called "defeatists" in our times.

Meanwhile the news was growing rapidly frightful. . . . We were told not to use the telephone if we could help it and we felt cut off and very ignorant.

"Meanwhile, round about this time, maybe a day or so later, odd news was beginning to creep in from Flinthannock and all along the coast. Unexpected people mentioned it, many of whom did not at first see its terrifying significance. The Government were collecting little boats and men to man them. What for? Things were as bad as that, were they?" She continues: "What a sporting chance, though! What a move! How like old Churchill! How tragically makeshift, but how traditional!"[44]

43. Ibid., 167, 154, 176, 187.

44. Ibid., 168, 175. The novelist Vera Brittain, around 15 May: "During the next few days, the beauty of England increases as the news gets steadily worse." On 19 May: "Again, as in the autumn, Martin and I, like other

In addition to such personal recollections, there exists another, rather valuable fund of sources of evidences of public opinion and popular sentiment in Britain at that time. These are the files of "Mass-Observation," or M-O, as it came to be known, preserved in the archives of the University of Sussex.[45] In the United States a milestone in the history of public opinion research was the establishment of the Gallup Institute in Princeton in 1935. Two years later two enterprising Englishmen, Charles Madge and Tom Harrisson ("who had come into 'people-watching' via his interest in bird-watching and natural history": Dorothy Sheridan), created M-O. They "began to recruit a nationwide panel of Observers to participate in a study of everyday life," mostly for commercial purposes, but in 1938 they expanded their scope to politics and war. In May 1940 they began to transmit materials and even give recommendations to the Ministry of Information. Unlike Gallup and other Americans engaged in public opinion research, they made no pretense to anything "scientific" and did not attempt to quantify all their data. That is exactly where the value of these materials resides. They are first-hand reports, typed by intelligent, commonsensical, mostly middle-class observers, many of them women volunteers. Even these many years later, their summaries breathe with the presence of authenticity and genuine concern.[46]

London householders, take the pictures off the walls, store our valuables in the basement, put buckets of sand in the passages, keep the bath filled with water, and make similar preparations. . . . This done, visit the hairdresser, deciding that if I must be bombed, I may as well be bombed with neatly arranged hair" (*England's Hour*, 30–31).

45. Directed by the excellent Dorothy Sheridan, still keeper of the archives.

46. The files in the University of Sussex Archives are well organized. For May 1940 "Morale Today" is a summary, Box DR 28, FR 124. It contains

Here, for example, are items from the closely typed, one-page summary of 16 May (FR 124, C 7, nine long paragraphs):

Exceptionally intensive investigation had been made today on the impact of latest news from Belgium and France. . . .

People have become distinctly more worried today. A proportion are now feeling desperate, though this does not mean that they think we shall not win in the end. A feeling of Hitler's superiority grows. . . .

Deeply concerned people are keeping up a good deal of optimism today, though all observers agree in finding that face and tone often belie the words. . . .

People haven't begun to consider that we might be actually beaten. It just hasn't occurred to most people that we *can* be beaten. The old complacency has been shaken, but it persists. If suddenly shattered, there will be a morale explosion.

Women are much more worried than men, and some are now showing definite terror of the immediate future. They are much more bewildered than men, and many are unable to grasp what is happening at all, especially working-class.

On 19 May "there is an improvement in tone today. Especially in London, but not in Lancashire."[47] "People remain confident that we will win in the long run, but today still shows plenty of implicit or unconscious defeatism, and a few open references to German victory."

That night — 19 May — Churchill first broadcast to the people

---

files from 18 May to 1 June, for every day: forty-three carefully drafted, typed reports from London, Bolton, Worcester, and Ipswich.

47. "A similar lag of about twenty-four hours in Lancashire reaction had been found in several previous crisis investigations."

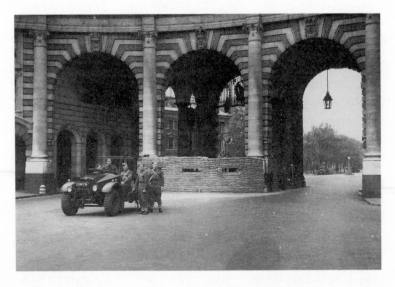

"A feeling of grave seriousness remains . . . " Admiralty Arch was fortified
to defend Whitehall against attack by German parachutists landing in
Trafalgar Square; beyond the Arch are the Admiralty and St. James's Park.

of Britain. The general reaction was favorable, mostly because of
his straightforward phrases about the gravity of the situation. On
20 May M-O "observers report that tension is slightly relieved today, . . . slightly less gloom, slightly more detachment about people's attitude to the news. . . . A feeling of grave seriousness remains,
if anything emphasized by Churchill's broadcast. . . . Women con-
spicuously more worried than men today. General feeling is that we
should pull through, just." On 21 May a very discerning observer
reports: "There is still no one view which can with any justice be
labelled 'public opinion' — it is too varied and unformed. The most
certain thing remains the belief that Britain will triumph eventually."

"Women remain, as usual, more pessimistic and less optimistic than men."

Next day, "unexpectedly," investigations "report that morale is down, or rather that anxiety is up."

Women are in a particularly depressed condition, and today for the first time, some are openly showing it. . . . On the other hand, many men and some women still feel confident that the situation is not really as bad as supposed, and comparisons with the last war are often brought up.

The fear that a Nazi invasion is *possible* is now beginning to appear.

The bewilderment and distress is more severe today than ever before, and the disillusion about all our past confidence and proud leadership is becoming a major strain on ordinary simple minds.

In *Bolton* people are much more calm than in London. Three investigators there made the following pertinent comment on this morning's detailed investigations: "The public is deliberately burying its head in the sands. This attitude is more common among the women." Londoners are more pessimistic.

"The result of the speeches given in the last few days by Churchill and Duff Cooper . . . is to engender a feeling of relief, not because the situation is not serious, but because the people feel they know the worst, which is a new experience for them."

It may be of some interest that many of the observers write about "feeling" rather than "thinking" (customary in English, of course, but perhaps worth noticing, given the overlap but still existing difference between opinions and sentiments). Thus, on 23 May, "a noticeable increase in cheerfulness and general calm, a distinct decrease in pessimism and extreme nervousness . . . for the time being. The intense gloom which affected many in London yesterday, mainly among the middle-classes, but also some of the working-classes, is not conspicuous today."

"The feeling that a big effort is going to be required and that our leaders are capable of asking for it . . . is growing. The feeling had a big value in liberating people from the general feeling of apathy, inactivity, and ineffectiveness which seriously depressed and worried a large number. . . . This new feeling is frequently reflected in verbatim material today, comments like 'We'll soon be doing something.' 'I'm prepared to do anything.' 'Well, everyone's in it now.'"

Nearly sixty years later a historian may attempt to sum up two general impressions. One is that on 23 May the majority of the British people did not know how catastrophic the situation of their army was. The other is that their confidence in Churchill was something of a new element, beginning to have something of an effect. Still, there can hardly be a better summation than the last sentence of the "Morale Today" report of 19 May: "'Outwardly calm, inwardly anxious' covers the general tone of today."

CHAPTER TWO

Friday, 24 May

Hitler's halt order. – The Germans before Dunkirk. – Calais. –
Hitler and the Conservatives. – The two Rights. – Chamberlain. –
Appeasers. – Halifax. – The War Cabinet. – Churchill and Roosevelt. –
The British press. – "A slight increase in anxiety and a
slight decrease in optimism."

Early on the morning of 24 May Hitler left his headquarters on
the edge of Germany and flew to see General Karl Rundstedt at
Charleville on the western bank of the Meuse. This was unusual,
since it was Hitler's custom to retire late and to rise late (it seems
that the last time he had got up early was on 3 September 1939, the
day of the British and French declarations of war on Germany).
What he wanted to discuss with Rundstedt was obviously important. It involved the rapid progress of the German armies encircling
the Allied army in Flanders and Belgium, pushing the latter to the
remaining ports on the Channel, where Boulogne had already fallen,
where the siege of Calais was about to begin, and where General

Guderian's armored troops were but fifteen miles to the south of Dunkirk, having crossed their widest obstacle, the Aa Canal, in two places. But there were dangers to consider: Guderian may have advanced too quickly. About this Hitler and Rundstedt seemed to agree. At 11:42 that morning the order went out: Guderian's advance must be temporarily halted.

There is a fair amount of literature (and speculation) about the sources (rather than about the consequences) of Hitler's halt order. Hitler's motives and purposes were not simple. We must attempt to sum them up — or, rather, to sort them out. On one level (if that is the proper phrase) of his mind he was concerned about the wear and tear on the German armored vehicles, in continuous movement and skirmishing for a fortnight now: this concern accorded with those of Rundstedt, who had made an account of such losses the night before. Perhaps this concern was also buttressed by Hitler's memories of the First World War, when he had served four long years in a land crisscrossed by watercourses and canals and where large armies attempted offensives mired in the mud. More evident, and documentable, are Hitler's nervous worries at the time. He still feared the possibility of an Allied counteroffensive maiming the snout of the advancing German crocodile. In sum, he did not — yet — believe his luck.

There was another element in his mind. Any historian worth his salt knows how to eschew monocausal explanations of human events — that is, the attribution of a single motive to any given decision.[1] And there is another necessary distinction, the one between motives and purposes (the first a push of the past, the second the pull

---

1. Bond, *Britain, France, and Belgium* (an excellent description of the confused planning and commitment of the Allies): "Hitler's motives were complex" (104).

of the future), for rare are also those instances when the purposes of a decision are singular or exclusive. This applies to Adolf Hitler, too, who was secretive and whose mind was not simple. It is at least possible that he wished not to annihilate the entire British Expeditionary Force. "Not to annihilate" is perhaps the phrase that comes closest to the truth, or, rather, to the workings of his mind. There are not a few instances, in war as in politics, when it is to the victor's advantage to let — or to force — his opponents to make a narrow escape, for otherwise, having burned their bridges, they may fight to the very end, with all kinds of unforeseeable consequences. That almost surely was in Hitler's mind. But he would soon in retrospect exaggerate his purposes. "Bridge" — indeed, "golden bridge" — are the words some Germans have used to explain Hitler's decision to halt before Dunkirk. These include Rundstedt, whose reminiscences do, however, have elements of special pleading. After the war Churchill, in his *War Memoirs,* took good care to ignore speculations about golden bridges; he attributed the halt order to Rundstedt's hesitations rather than to Hitler's. Churchill was not altogether incorrect: "golden bridge" was an overstatement, to say the least. But an overstatement, while wanting in precision, is not necessarily altogether devoid of truth. Other people in Hitler's circle heard him say, "The Führer wants to spare the British a humiliating defeat."[2] After Dunkirk came Hitler's rationalization: "The army is England's backbone. . . . If we destroy it, there goes the British Empire. We would not, or could not, inherit it. . . . My generals did not understand this."[3] And near the end of the war, in February 1945: "Churchill was quite unable to appreciate the sporting spirit of which I

2. General of the Luftwaffe Hans Jeschonnek on 26 May, quoted in Ansel, *Hitler Confronts England,* 85.

3. His secretary, Christa Schroeder, in *Er War mein Chef,* 105.

have given proof by refraining from creating an irreparable breach between the British and ourselves. We did, however, refrain from annihilating them at Dunkirk."[4]

Hitler's purposes were mixed. He wanted the British army to leave Europe. But by "not annihilating" the BEF, he did not wish to spare them. Three days before the halt order he let himself be convinced by Hermann Goering that the retreating BEF could be smashed to pieces by the Luftwaffe. On 23 May Major Engel, Hitler's adjutant, noted in his diary that Hitler and Goering were talking on the telephone again: "The Field Marshal thinks that the great task of the Luftwaffe is beginning: the annihilation of the British in Northern France. The army will only have to occupy. We are angry. The Führer is inspired."[5] Another diary entry of 23 May, this one by the canny Ernst von Weizsaecker, undersecretary of state: "Whether the English give in now or whether we make them peace-loving through bombing . . . " Well, the bombing did not work. The halt order was crucial: "Dunkirk is to be left to the Luftwaffe. Should the capture of Calais prove difficult, this port too is to be left to the Luftwaffe."

Hitler's halt order was sent in clear.[6] It was instantly read in London. (It was brought to the command in the War Office by General A. E. Percival, assistant chief of defence of the general staff — the unfortunate man who, less than two years later, would be the feeble defender of Singapore, surrendering it to the Japanese: the most shameful defeat of British arms in an entire century.) Neither the War Office nor Churchill nor Lord Gort, the commander of the BEF,

4. *The Testament of Adolf Hitler,* 90.

5. Engel Diary, 23 May.

6. Is it at least possible that Hitler did not mind the British overhearing it? Possible, yes; probable, no.

recognized its immediate importance.[7] The confusion in the War Office was great and deep. They were preoccupied with the situation at Calais. Boulogne had capitulated to the Germans the night before. At 2 A.M. an order was sent to Calais: "evacuation was decided in principle." The siege of Calais was about to begin; in the morning the first German artillery shells began to pepper the port. Two large British ships, loaded with British troops, cast off from Calais for Dover. The Germans could see this with their own eyes. The British were leaving the Continent. This may have contributed to Hitler's halt order. A few minutes before the halt order, Brigadier Claude Nicholson, the British commander at Calais, told the War Office by telephone that evacuation would continue. He expected it to be completed some time the next day. Somewhat later the War Office countermanded the evacuation plan: Calais was to be held as long as possible. Often through that afternoon British and French troops, marching to vessels at the port, were turned around with orders to stay in Calais. The confusion at the War Office was worse than what was happening in Calais. Earlier that day Churchill had learned of the evacuation order. He minuted to General Ismay: "This is surely madness. The only effect of evacuating Calais would be to transfer the forces now blocking it to Dunkirk. Calais must be held for many reasons, but especially to hold the enemy, on its front."[8] By noon Churchill's impetuosity got the better of him. Again he sent a note to Ismay: "I cannot understand the situation

7. However, General Pownall noted (*Chief of Staff*, 337): "An intercept German message in clear, timed 11:32 [in reality, 11:42], that the attack on the Line Dunkirk-Hazebrouck-Merville is to be discontinued for the present. Can this be the turn of the tide? It seems almost too much to hope for. [Yes.] . . . Of course these Germans are about all in, that's certain. [No.]."
8. CA, 4/150.

around Calais. . . . The Germans are blocking all exits. . . . Yet I expect [the German] forces achieving this are very modest. Why then are they not attacked? Why does not Lord Gort attack them from the rear at the same time that we make a sortie from Calais?" This seemed logical to Churchill: another, smaller version of a two-pronged attack, cutting off the German snout. In reality, it made no sense at all.[9] As Airey Neave, who had fought and was wounded and captured at Calais (and who later escaped from a German prison camp), afterward put it, "Churchill's admonition to Gort to attack the Tenth Panzer Division when the B.E.F. was separated from Calais by at least four Panzer Divisions . . . [is] evidence of the terrifying ignorance of those conducting this campaign from Whitehall."[10]

There was another reason to hold on to Calais. The French pressed the British to stay on, not to evacuate. Indeed it may have seemed to the French that the British were packing up, leaving them in the lurch. Churchill was sufficiently appreciative of this, because of its political — and human — implications. General Weygand had ordered to maintain a large connected bridgehead: the ports "can be held for a long time." That was an unreasonable exaggeration. Yet Calais did hold out till the afternoon of the twenty-sixth, and that made a difference. Had Calais not been defended, two other German divisions would have joined Guderian pushing northward. He was already on the north side of the Aa Canal before Dunkirk; on the twenty-fourth there were only a small British corps and a few French units between him and Dunkirk. "Had this happened," Neave later wrote, "there would have been no need for Hitler's

9. See Pownall on Churchill that day ("The man is mad," above). This violent criticism, however, was aimed not at the above dispatch but at Churchill's earlier endorsement of the larger, so-called Weygand plan.

10. CA 4/150; Neave, *The Flames of Calais*, 122–23.

intervention *which lost Guderian the historic chance of winning the Second World War almost in a morning.*"[11] The italics are mine. There may be some imprecision — imprecision, rather than exaggeration — in Neave's statement: but not much.[12]

There was now, at least temporarily, a difference between the War Office and Churchill. The command in London wished to save the British units in Calais. They therefore still would have preferred evacuation, while Churchill wanted to fight on in Calais till the end — partly, as we have seen, because of its effects on the French, but also partly because, as he properly recognized, it would slow down the German advance to the last port, Dunkirk. The War Office was constrained to agree with Churchill, though with some reluctance. This appears from the telegram that the War Office sent to Brigadier Nicholson late (at 11:23 P.M.) on 24 May: "In spite of policy of evacuation given you this morning fact that British forces in your area now under Fagalde [General Fagalde was a courageous French commander in the Calais area] who has ordered no repeat no evacuation means that you comply for the sake of Allied solidarity." When Churchill read this early next morning, he was furious. He sent a message to General Ironside: "Pray find out who was the officer responsible for sending the order to evacuate Calais yesterday and by whom this very lukewarm telegram I saw this morning was drafted in which mention is made of 'for the sake of Allied

11. Neave, *The Flames of Calais,* 107.

12. I say imprecision, because at the time of Hitler's halt order, Guderian's spearheads across the Aa Canal were not advancing; they were consolidating their bridgeheads. On the other hand, had Hitler or Rundstedt ordered Guderian to proceed with his advance toward Dunkirk, there is reason to believe that he would have arrived there in a day's march, well before a considerable number of Allied troops, retreating from the east, would have got to the town.

Solidarity? This is no way to encourage men to fight to the end. Are you sure there is no streak of defeatist opinion in General Staff?" There *was* at least a small streak of defeatist opinion in Ironside, to whom this fast minute was directed. Even though there were no signs of defeatism among the officers and soldiers of the British units under Gort (still well to the east of Dunkirk, retreating slowly westward), signs of defeatism were apparent in the Belgian army, where some of the Flemish soldiers were unwilling to fight Germans. In any event, when Churchill read the "lukewarm telegram" early on the morning of the twenty-fifth, the swastika flag was already flying on the Hôtel de Ville in Calais. Around the port and the maritime quays Nicholson and Fagalde held out, for another day and a half.

◆ ◆ ◆

This is not a military history of May 1940. But it is not reasonable or even possible to separate the unfolding of the military from the political sequence of events. Nor is it at all reasonable to separate Hitler's military purposes from his political ones. Their essences were the same: to convince the British not to oppose him, certainly not in Europe. Were they to leave the Continent, all to the good; he might have to force them to do that; but they ought not be dead set to fight him at any cost. Now there was Churchill; but he was not "the British."

This is not the place to attempt a detailed analysis of Hitler's understanding of the British. He had a certain respect for their Empire and also for their soldierly abilities (especially because of what he had seen during the First World War). He knew something, but not much, about their history. He did not really understand the common people of Britain or elements of their character. But as the war proceeded, his respect for the British faded fast. He began to deprecate their fighting abilities, and toward the end of the war he turned on them with a furious hatred — his rocket firings at London and many of his statements are evidences of that. He blamed the British for having chosen to oppose him and thus, like the Poles, having precipitated the war.

But this was May 1940. What he saw then (and he had agreed with Joseph Goebbels when the latter had said something like this in April) was that this was but a repetition, on a larger scale, of the struggle that he had fought and won in Germany, which had brought him to power. He and his National Socialists were bound to win the struggle, even though they had started out as a minority, because they and their ideas were more determined and stronger than those of their opponents. That during the street fighting in Weimar Germany a National Socialist trooper was worth two or three of his Communist or Socialist opponents was a consequence of that. During the war Hitler believed that, much in the same way, one German soldier was worth two or three Polish or French or perhaps even British soldiers, not only because of superior German discipline and equipment but also because a German soldier of the Third Reich incarnated a national ideology that was better and stronger than those of his enemies. And thus 80 million Germans were more than a match for their nearly 100 million Western European opponents, with all their many empires behind them. There was some truth in this but not enough. In the end 80 million Germans, tough match as they were, were not enough to withstand the hundreds of millions of Russians and Americans and British and others pouring over them. But that was not yet so in May 1940.

There was another element in Hitler's vision about this war being but a larger repetition of his struggle in Germany a decade or so before. There he could not have come to power without the support of the German Conservatives. In 1923 he had attempted a radical nationalist uprising in Munich, challenging the established authorities if need be. It failed, and thereafter he changed his mind or, rather, his tactics. He would come to power with the support of the Conservative parties, of their politicians, of their press, and of the masses of respectable conservative German voters. They would support him not only because they would be impressed with his mass following. They would be inclined to sympathize, at least to some extent, with his nationalism, with his anti-Semitism, and especially with his anti-Communism. Thus he would disarm their opposition; he would gain a certain amount of respectability and their support when needed. They would think that he was dependent on them, that he was their partner; but, once in power, *they* would be entirely dependent on *him,* and soon. This was, of course, what happened in Germany in 1933. He had little respect for these people; indeed, he regarded most of them (and on occasion said so) with contempt. A prototypical example of such German Conservatives was Alfred Hugenberg, the Nationalist party leader and press magnate, with whom Hitler made an alliance in 1930 and whom Hitler discarded easily a few months after his assumption of power, having no trouble with the erstwhile Hugenbergers, most of them *his* followers now.

And then, beginning at the latest in 1935, when his relationship with Britain became very important to him, he met people among the British governing classes, members of the British aristocracy, and the British Conservative Party; he met Halifax, and then Chamberlain, and many others, too, including the old Lloyd George — and again, Hitler saw, or thought he saw, through them, as indeed he had seen through so many opponents and followers during his extraordinary career. He thought that he understood their strengths and their weaknesses, just as he had understood his potential German conservative opponents before 1933. And just as these German Conservatives were unwilling to take a firm stand against Hitler (certainly unwilling to station themselves on the side of liberals, socialists, or other leftists), it was evident that these Britishers were unwilling to consider a war with him, certainly not on the side of the

French or of other Europeans. Just as these German Conservatives feared Communism and took comfort in Hitler's evidently uncompromising anti-Communism and anti-Marxism, so did some of these British Conservatives. Indeed, just as some of these German Conservatives had done, they seemed to be willing to give him the benefit of the doubt and to see his New Order as at least an alternative both to Communism and to the decaying and corrupting climate of an antiquated parliamentary liberalism. Hitler did not sufficiently understand that Britons were not Germans — that the patriotism of British Conservatives and the nationalism of German Konservatives were not quite the same things. But when he occasionally called the British appeasers "meine Hugenberger," my Hugenbergers, he was not entirely wrong.

♦ ♦ ♦

We have seen that many — probably the majority — of the Conservative members in the House of Commons did not particularly like Churchill and that their reluctance to applaud him was largely due to their uneasiness with his personal and public reputation, with his past. There was, however, more to it than that. These members of Parliament — a huge Conservative majority — were elected in 1935, and in 1935 the policies of the government, the inclinations of their party and what seems to have been those of the majority of the British people, were not what they were in 1940. In 1935 and for some years thereafter, they were willing — more precisely, they were not unwilling — to give the new Germany a measure of credit. Since then at least a dozen books have been written about appeasement. This is not the place to compose another précis of its history. Besides, "appeasement," as such, was a dead issue in 1940, when Britain and Germany were at war. But the uncertain acceptance — indeed, the lack of enthusiasm for Churchill in May 1940 — had much to do with his anti-appeasement record and rhetoric, including his many attacks on Chamberlain's policy that stopped only in September

1939 — which is why we cannot avoid a short description of the inclinations of Churchill's former (and in May 1940 still latent) opponents.

The British tendency to appease Germany (the term "appeasement" did not become widely current until later, in 1938) had many sources. They included the gradual recognition of the British people that Germany had been treated unfairly by the Treaty of Versailles and thereafter. There was the almost universal wish of government and people (shared by Labour and pacifists) to avoid a British involvement in another war, especially another war in Europe, at almost any cost. To these wide and popular inclinations was added the willingness of many Conservatives and at least a portion of the upper classes to give some credit to the then-new types of authoritarian governments in Europe, largely owing to their seemingly determined anti-Communism. As Andrew Roberts wrote in his biography of Halifax: "Although today it is considered shameful and craven, the policy of appeasement once occupied almost the whole moral high ground. The word was originally synonymous with idealism, magnanimity of the victor and the willingness to right wrongs."[13] Pragmatism rather than idealism, we might say, and an unwillingness to risk involvement rather than magnanimity, but Roberts is not altogether wrong. He is certainly right in citing Sir Samuel Hoare that in March 1936 there was "a strong pro-German feeling in this country" and that the then prime minister Stanley Baldwin feared war, since that "would probably only result in Germany going Bolshevik."[14] (Churchill and others — both before and

13. Roberts, *The Holy Fox,* 49.

14. Ibid., 59. See also Pownall, who respected Hitler at that time: a "pronounced Anti-German complex . . . I regard as a danger to the country" (*Chief of Staff,* 93).

well after the war — declared that the last chance to deter Hitler was to move against him when he reoccupied the Rhineland in March 1936, as if that would have been an easy thing. They were wrong.)

There exists a photograph of Baldwin and Chamberlain walking together to Parliament in early 1937. Their clothes are black and rumpled; with their stiff high collars, umbrella, and cane, Baldwin topped with a high bowler, Chamberlain with a shiny top hat, they look like surviving incarnations of an entirely outdated Victorianism — as outdated as Hugenberg or Hindenburg or Schacht in 1933 or 1934, when seen (and not only when read), and in contrast to the Hitler of "The Triumph of the Will"; prototypical figures of an old — though not *very* old — Right.

We must understand that the great conflict of the 1930s, of the period before June 1941 (when Hitler invaded the Soviet Union) and even well after that in many places, was not between Right and Left but, rather, one between two Rights. In one sense, "Right" and "Left" were becoming less and less useful as categories or definitions. Was Hitler to the Right or to the Left of Churchill? Either of these designations would be incorrect. Hitler was a revolutionary and not a traditionalist, but in many ways he superseded these increasingly antiquated categories. More important, for our purposes, was the recognition that throughout the 1930s, especially in Europe, the Left was weak. Except for the Soviet Union, there was no Communist regime anywhere on the globe; except for small minorities and some intellectuals, Communism did not attract masses of people. In Germany the socialist and Communist opposition to Hitler melted away in the sun of his National Socialist successes, and this was not very different from what happened in other nations. In England, too, support for the Labour Party did not really increase even after most Labourites abandoned their more or less traditional pacifism and opposed appeasement. The most principled opponents

"Baldwin [right] and Chamberlain walking together to Parliament in early
1937. Their clothes are black and rumpled; with their stiff high collars,
umbrella, and cane, Baldwin topped with a high bowler, Chamberlain with
a shiny top hat, they look like surviving incarnations of an entirely
outdated Victorianism . . . "

of Hitler and the Third Reich were traditionalist patriots like Churchill or de Gaulle — and, in Germany, the handful of aristocratic conspirators who finally tried to kill Hitler in 1944. In Britain the real chasm existed between Churchill and his followers on one side and Chamberlain and his followers on the other; in France, between de Gaulle and Pétain; in Italy and in Spain, too, between fascists and royalists. In these as in many other European countries, the main conflict was between Right and Right rather than between Right and Left. (In the United States, too, the most dangerous and popular challengers of Franklin Roosevelt were men of the Right, not of the Left: Huey Long and Father Coughlin.) In one sense, it may be said, the division was between patriots and nationalists, or between traditionalists and pragmatists — but we must not let ourselves get involved in a sump of definitions. Perhaps it would be closer to the truth to say that the division was between reactionaries and conservatives; indeed, on many occasions Churchill was criticized as a "hopeless reactionary" or an "extreme rightist," and not only by Hitlerites or by Communists but by many of the Chamberlain conservatives (which is why I wrote that Chamberlain did represent an old, but not very old, Right). Was Chamberlain to the Right or to the Left of Churchill? Both designations are arguable, but perhaps we should rest with the wisdom of Samuel Johnson, to the effect that "definitions are tricks for pedants."[15]

In any event: in the 1930s Neville Chamberlain was prototypical, the leading figure of British conservatism. His reputation was "steady" (very much unlike that of Churchill before 1940). He was

---

15. While some saw (and some still see) Churchill as a reactionary, others saw him as a pro-democratic demagogue. Sheila Lawlor, in *Churchill and the Politics of War:* "Churchill and his supporters . . . were the radicals fighting forces of reaction" (4). This is quite wrong.

steady in his dislike of flamboyance, of intellectualism, of extremism, of irresponsibilities political or fiscal — steady in his narrow but strong vision of the path that Britain must take and follow. He was steady in his abhorrence of war,[16] of Communists and leftists, of the Soviet Union, of press propaganda; steady in his unwillingness to become involved in European politics and in his distrust of the French (and of Americans); and, consequent to all this, steady in his willingness to grant the Germans, including Hitler, a more than considerable benefit of the doubt. That last inclination may have been fortified by two other elements in his mental makeup, one late Victorian, the other modern. His Midland, nonconformist, Victorian tendency to trust Germans rather than French was not unlike that of his father, the master politician Joseph Chamberlain, who in 1899 had proposed that the world ought to be governed by the Teutonic nations: Britain, America, Germany. More timely, in the 1930s, was Chamberlain's recognition of the failure of parliamentary-liberal democracy in many countries, though not of course in England. He, as indeed did many others (including Churchill),[17] saw the new kind of order established by Mussolini (and, in Chamberlain's case, even the one by Hitler) as having certain positive features, especially their determined anti-Communism. Chamberlain, unlike Churchill, did

16. Pownall wrote in 1936: Chamberlain is "entirely ignorant about military and strategic questions. . . . His ideas on strategy would disgrace a board school" (*Chief of Staff*, 42). Consider, too, Roberts: "The senior anti-appeasers all had fine war records — Duff Cooper, Anthony Eden, Harold Macmillan, Winston Churchill, Roger Keyes, Louis Spears and so on — while National government ministers who advocated appeasement — Baldwin, Macdonald, Chamberlain, Hoare, Sir John Simon, Sir Kingsley Wood — had not themselves seen action" (*Eminent Churchillians,* 12).

17. See, among other evidences, his 1930 preface to *Dictatorship on Trial,* mentioned in Lukacs, *The Duel,* 51.

not have a quick mind (which is not always a handicap), but this meant that he was unwilling to change his mind about matters even after contrary evidence had begun to accumulate. Chamberlain's opponents therefore regarded him as small-minded and obstinate; his supporters as steady and stubborn — and for many years there were many more of the latter.

But in 1939 Chamberlain was forced to change his views — because of Hitler. His opponents thought that he was changing his mind too late; his supporters did not think so. We need not concern ourselves with that. But a change of mind does not mean (or, at least, very seldom means) a change in character. He was not made to be a war leader. He was, as Churchill would say at Chamberlain's funeral in November 1940, "an English worthy," and so he was in August 1939, when he knew that Britain must keep its word and go to war, however reluctantly. Yet on 23 August 1939 — the day when the news of Hitler's pact with Stalin had come and the day when Hitler gave the order to set the day for the invasion of Poland — Chamberlain said to the American ambassador Joseph Kennedy, "I have done everything that I can think of and it seems as if all my work has come to naught." According to Kennedy, Chamberlain was deeply depressed: "[He] says the futility of it all is the thing that is frightful; after all they cannot save the Poles; they can merely carry on a war of revenge that will mean the destruction of the whole of Europe."[18] (Chamberlain also, at least partially, shared Kennedy's anti-Semitism.)[19] There followed the eight months of the Reluctant

18. Aster, *1939*, 334–35. It is not improbable that Kennedy may have exaggerated. These are Kennedy's words; he tried to convince Chamberlain to pressure the Poles to give in.

19. Kennedy to James Forrestal, December 1945: "Chamberlain, he says, stated that America and the world Jews had forced England into the war"

War. Chamberlain was still prime minister. "The fact that the early stages of the war were ones of inactivity was not merely because there was little that could be done, but in addition because Chamberlain wanted little to be done."[20] That was why Churchill succeeded him, on 10 May, after the debate in the House of Commons when a portion of conservative members had temporarily deserted Chamberlain, though without really conferring their full allegiance on Churchill.

But in addition to supporters of Chamberlain and to the conservative majority in Parliament, there were other influential elements in the ranks of government and society whose dislike of Churchill did not of course vanish entirely in May 1940. Extreme elements — such as the Mosleyites, British Fascists, Germano-maniacs, obsessive anti-Semites, and so on — were without considerable influence, and, as we shall see, by 24 May they were safely put away by the government through the instrument of a draconian regulation about which Chamberlain fully concurred with Churchill. But in Britain (unlike almost anywhere else in Europe), there were many members of the aristocracy who, at least before May 1940, expressed their rather definite sympathies for Hitler — or, at least, for the then-

---

(*Forrestal Diaries*, 122). Kenneth Clark, who was fairly close to Chamberlain, wrote in his memoir *Another Part of the Wood: A Self-Portrait* (a very carefully crafted self-portrait) that Chamberlain had told him at Chequers that "he was a man of facts." Clark: "Were not Hitler's speeches and the horrors of Nazidom facts? Mr. Chamberlain closed his mind to them. 'All propaganda,' he said, when I ventured to mention them to him" (270–71). (Has Clark "ventured" to do that? Perhaps.)

20. "This was a state of affairs happily concurred with, although for different reasons, by the French government" (Esnouf, "British Government War Aims and Attitudes," 30).

Germanophile inclinations of Chamberlain.[21] Such tendencies were shared by members of the royal family and, what was more important, by high civil servants of considerable influence.[22] One of these was Sir Horace Wilson, who before 1940 was Chamberlain's closest and most trusted adviser. R. A. Butler, in a letter in 1939, somewhat facetiously referred to Wilson as "the uncrowned ruler of England." The reminiscences of Kenneth Clark would seem to support Butler's assessment: "Mr Chamberlain was not an imaginative man and was singularly devoid of 'antennae.' Decisions involving these qualities

21. As late as April 1939 "Halifax was deluged with letters from a number of the nation's grandest aristocrats imploring him to return to appeasement. Althought they differed over details, their general line was that Germany bore no ill will towards Britain per se and ought to be allowed a free path eastwards to fight Russia. To these people the Polish guarantee was a disastrous error. Another constantly recurring feature in the letters was the belief that war with Germany would be ruinous to Britain's place in the world and only Jews and Communists would benefit. Halifax, who had himself roughly subscribed to almost these views as recently as 1937–38, wrote back long and polite letters, courteously explaining and defending his policy. He knew these correspondents socially; indeed, he had been the Marquis of Londonderry's fag at Eton. [Some of them] still implored him, well after the war had begun, to review friendship with Germany" (Roberts, *The Holy Fox*, 151–52).

22. The evidences of this are not easy to reconstruct, since they are scattered and of course incomplete. (There is much interesting material in Roberts, *Eminent Churchillians*.) Chamberlain did not weed his papers and correspondence (in Birmingham University Library), or at least not much. Halifax (in the Borthwick Institute Library of the University of York) did so more considerably, as did Lady Halifax. In the Churchill Archives, Cambridge, the diaries of Sir Maurice Hankey have been culled: there is either nothing or very little for each year of the period 1939–44, though some of his correspondence is there. In the papers of David Margesson, the chief whip

were made for him by an extraordinary character called Sir Horace Wilson. He sat in a small office outside the Prime Minister's room in Downing Street, and everyone with an appointment had to pass through this office and have a few minutes' conversation with Sir Horace. . . . I enjoyed my occasional conversations with him, and said so to Mr Chamberlain. His eyes lit up, he turned to look at me and said: 'He is the most remarkable man in England. I couldn't live a day without him.'"[23] After 10 May he had to: one of the first things that Churchill did was to tell Horace Wilson to get out.

R. A. Butler was Halifax's undersecretary at the Foreign Office and, in some ways, Halifax's Wilson, though Halifax was less dependent on Butler than Chamberlain had been on Wilson. Like Wilson,

---

of the Conservatives (deposited in the Churchill Archives by his daughter), the years 1939–46 are missing. Weeded, too, are the Butler Papers in Trinity College, Cambridge: the "Guide" to these papers states, for example, "Four items appear to be of continuing sensitivity and should not be made available until that sensitivity can be said to have evaporated." (These items are in E 3/60, a batch of letters to and from Sir Samuel Hoare and Wing Commander Archie James, MP, at the British Embassy in Madrid.)

23. Butler to Lord Brabourne, 17 February 1939, Butler Papers, F 79/93. Clark, *Another Part of the World,* 271. Also Butler Papers, F 80/98 (written mid-1939): "I have always attempted to do a character study of those with whom I have worked. . . . Sir Horace Wilson's power is very great. He is the Burleigh of the present age and he interested me very much the other day when he compared the task of Chamberlain to that of Queen Elizabeth. . . . [He] likes power and 'moves in a mysterious way his wonders to perform.' . . . His forte of industrial negotiation will be stretched to the utmost if he is ever able to come to an understanding with Nazi Germany as he still in his heart hopes to do so. . . . [But] it would be unfair to say that this notable figure with his blue eyes, soft voice and furtive face, is the architect only of appeasement."

Butler was a consummate intriguer and wire-puller. He was also rich and a believer in social hierarchy, in a compound of aristocracy mixed with some democracy as being the essence of Britain. One indication of his inclinations may be gathered from his handwritten letter to Chamberlain and Halifax on 18 March 1938, only a few days after Hitler's invasion and annexation of Austria, recommending an account by E. W. D. Tennant, chairman of the Anglo-German Fellowship: "He is quite discreet and sincere. . . . I am not telling him that I have shown this to you and Halifax." Tennant's "account" (here and there laced with anti-Jewish remarks) accused the hapless Austrian chancellor Kurt von Schuschnigg of having imposed "brutal cruelties" on the Austrian Nazis. Its essence:

> England is still mainly governed by an aristocracy with ancient traditions basically unchanged for centuries. Germany is governed by one comparatively young man risen from low beginnings with no personal experience of other countries and surrounded by advisers of similar type, all men of vital, dynamic energy who have gone through an incredibly hard school, . . . who are tough, ruthless but immensely able and who believe themselves to be governed by very high ideals. I still believe that it should not only be possible, but easy, to make friends with them. . . . Hitler is determined as ever by any means, fair or even foul, to prevent Communism overrunning Europe.

To this Butler added: "I think you will find his account remarkably true."[24]

Like Horace Wilson, who pulled many kinds of wires (at least in one case literally — he was behind the tapping of Winston Churchill's telephone conversations in 1938), Butler had a talent for intriguing.

24. Ibid., F 70/14.

In April 1938 he devised a plan to influence the British press, "aware of the German anger at some [of the British papers]." "What we really want to organize is a little publicity committee for our work in the Foreign Office: . . . (a) see that our case [of appeasing Germany] is well represented, (b) see that the correspondence columns everywhere are well stacked with arguments written by our friends, (c) see that our speeches are better (as well) heard and known to our opponents' or semi-opponents', e.g. Winston's campaign should be watched."[25] When it came to appeasement, Butler was closer to Chamberlain than to his chief, Halifax; on occasion he even said so. "He took to appeasement with an unholy glee not shared after *Anschluss* by anyone else in the Foreign Office. His extreme partisanship against members of his own party, his relish for back-room deals and his almost messianic opposition to Churchill make Butler, as even his heavily weeded papers are unable to prevent, seem a thoroughly unattractive figure."[26]

Enough of this. During the Black Fortnight neither Wilson nor Butler were dramatis personae. On 11 May 1940 Churchill got rid of Horace Wilson. But he did not, because he could not, get rid of R. A. Butler in Whitehall. This was significant, because Butler was, after all, Halifax's undersecretary of state, and by 24 May a new alignment had begun to appear in the War Cabinet. Churchill's principal opponent was not Chamberlain; it was Halifax.

♦ ♦ ♦

Edward Wood, Lord Halifax, is the subject of an excellent biography by Andrew Roberts — superbly proportioned and composed, with a very impressive variety of sources. Valuable portions of it deal with Halifax's relations with Chamberlain and with Churchill.[27]

25. Ibid., F 79/24.
26. Roberts, *The Holy Fox,* 140.
27. Halifax's autobiography, *Fulness of Days,* is bland and hardly useful,

Since that triangular relationship was crucial to the events of May 1940, we must, at the risk of imprecision, essay a short sketch of Halifax's character and his career leading up to the Black Fortnight and eventually to his decision to oppose Churchill.

This is not easy. The personality of Halifax was very much unlike that of Churchill, but he was also unlike Chamberlain. His appearance was unusual: very tall, very gaunt and erect, he had a stance marked by his unusually large, splayed feet; he was born without a left hand, the prosthetic substitution for which (a fist) he managed exquisitely, as indeed he wore his unobtrusive but exquisitely cut clothes. His aristocratic appearance accorded well with his character: calm and cool, perhaps even cold; shy rather than sensitive; always in control of his emotions and, perhaps more admirably, of his ambitions. He had a faint (rather than weak) sense of humor, an English quality of which Chamberlain had almost none and Churchill (at least so it seemed to some people) had perhaps too much. His main interests — indeed, addictions — were foxhunting, High Anglicanism, and high government service. The first ran to such an extent that he would often use hunting and shooting figures of speech when wishing to illustrate quite different and even weighty matters; as for the second, he was the quintessential churchman, rather than an introspective man of faith; as to the third, "his career [was] an uninterrupted tale of achievement and promotion."[28] Churchill called him the Holy Fox, which, according to Roberts, was "a rather weak pun" (we do not think so). Perhaps the highest of his honors was his viceroyalty of India (as Lord Irwin), from 1925 to 1931; he was instrumental in the offer of dominion status to India, which Churchill violently opposed. After his return from

---

though here and there it does have touches of humor. The Earl of Birkenhead, *Halifax: The Life of Lord Halifax,* is more useful and at times critical.

28. Roberts, *The Holy Fox,* 1.

India Halifax was offered the foreign secretaryship in Ramsay Mac-
Donald's National Government, which he refused. He became Viscount Halifax on the death of his father in 1934 and accepted high
positions in the Baldwin and Chamberlain governments. For five
months in 1935 he was secretary of state for war — opposing rearma-
ment. In February 1938, as we saw, Chamberlain dismissed Anthony Eden and appointed Halifax as his foreign secretary.

Halifax was an appeaser — indeed, a quintessential, if not an altogether extreme, one. This is not the place to cite his many unfortunate and lamentable judgments about Hitler's Germany in the years
before and during most of 1938; there are innumerable examples of
these in his biographies, in those of his opponents, and in various
private papers and in public archives. "If not altogether extreme":
because in his particular case there are evidences when his proverbial
coolness and calmness of judgment were overpowered by illusions,
when in that otherwise so determinedly pragmatic mind his wishes
were the father of his thoughts — indeed, they *were* his thoughts,
as when he found Goering "frankly attractive" and Goebbels very
"likable." His understanding of Hitler was for a long time very wanting. On one occasion he compared Hitler's "mysticism" to that of
Gandhi. Upon his return from his most unfortunate meeting with
Hitler in November 1937, he wrote to Chamberlain that the colo-
nial issue was "the only vital question" remaining between Germany
and Britain. This was a vast misreading, not only of Hitler but of the
entire world situation.[29] Hitler's main ambitions were in Europe,

29. Ibid., 67, quoting from Baldwin's papers (173/61) on 15 November
1937: "The visit to Hitler constituted the high-water mark of Halifax's
appeasement." Writing to Baldwin of a recent conversation that the League
of Nations' commissioner of Danzig, Karl Burckhardt, had had with Hitler,
he remarked, "Nationalism and Racialism is a powerful force but I can't feel

not elsewhere. But then Halifax — this was one of the things he had in common with Chamberlain — was not much interested in Europe. That is why Churchill had his sleepless night after Chamberlain dismissed Eden and appointed Halifax. There is a typical Halifaxian reaction to Hitler's annexation of Austria in March 1938: "Was any useful purpose served by treading on the landslide and being carried along with it?"[30] There is a significant coincidence to this phrase. We shall see that on 27 May 1940 Churchill would choose a similar figure of speech, but one with a very contrary implication: when he told Halifax and the War Cabinet that any suggestion of an attempt to negotiate with Hitler would mean that Britain was stepping onto a "slippery slope." Roberts cites Oliver Harvey as saying, in 1938, that Halifax "easily blinds himself to unpleasant facts and is ingenious and even jesuitical in rounding awkward corners of his mind," but Roberts adds that Harvey's "damning assertion" was incorrect.[31] Yet during the spring and summer of 1938 Halifax was not above engaging in many kinds of clandestine contacts and trickeries, including attempts to manipulate the press and some strange statements made to intermediaries of Hitler.[32]

---

that it's either unnatural or immoral!" He added, on the eve of his departure, "I cannot myself doubt that these fellows are genuine haters of Communism, etc.! And I daresay if we were in their position we might feel the same!" When Ribbentrop, then the German ambassador in London, told Tom Jones, then an arch-appeaser, "The sooner Halifax met the Führer the better" (ibid., 64), he was right.

30. CAB 27/623–26 (378).

31. Roberts, *The Holy Fox,* 95.

32. As early as March 1936 (the Rhineland crisis) Halifax suggested that "any direct approach to Germany should be kept secret from the French" (ibid., 59). In July 1938 Hitler's adjutant, Captain Fritz Wiedemann, visited

On a night in September 1938 there came a change. On the fifteenth, Chamberlain suddenly flew to Berchtesgaden to meet Hitler,
seeking an agreement with him—an unprecedented journey by a
British prime minister. He had the full support of Halifax, as he did
again a week later, when Chamberlain flew to Hitler again, this time
to Godesberg, where Hitler ratcheted up his demands and showed
his ability to threaten. Loath to make any British commitment to
Czechoslovakia and France, Chamberlain was willing, perhaps even
eager, to go along with what Hitler wanted. There was a cabinet
meeting after Chamberlain's return. Halifax supported Chamberlain to the hilt. His undersecretary Alec Cadogan wrote in his diary:
"Still more horrified to find [Chamberlain] had hypnotized [Hali-
fax] who capitulates totally. . . . I gave [Halifax] a note of what *I*
thought, but it had no effect." There were two cabinets that evening;
after the second "[Halifax] completely and quite happily defeatist-
pacifist. . . . Drove him home and gave him a bit of my mind, but
didn't shake him."[33] Well, he did shake his mind. Next morning he
told Cadogan: "Alec, I'm very angry with you. You gave me a sleepless night. I woke at 1 and never got to sleep again. But I came to the

London. Halifax received him in his office. As he left, Halifax was supposed
to have said that he "would like to see as the culmination of his work the
Führer entering London at the side of the King amid the acclamations of the
English people." Wiedemann, who was not unreliable, reported this to
Hitler. It is found in the published volumes of the German diplomatic
documents and is also cited by Roberts, *Eminent Churchillians,* 16–17
(where, however, the visit is misdated as July 1939, not 1938); but Roberts
adds, "It is always possible that the statement was exaggerated, but when
the conversation was made public after the war, Halifax made no attempt to
deny it." Halifax's statement was also confirmed to this author (Private
information).

33. *Diaries of Sir Alexander Cadogan,* 103, 105.

conclusion that you were right." So, almost exactly seven months from the day when his appointment to the foreign secretaryship had given a sleepless night to Churchill, Halifax had *his* sleepless night. At the next cabinet he suddenly spoke up. Hitler was not to be trusted; eventually Nazism had to be eliminated. Chamberlain was stunned and disappointed. Later that day Halifax told Chamberlain about his sleepless night. Chamberlain answered him acidly, with a humorless sally about the dubious value of night thoughts. But from that time on there was a divergence between Chamberlain's and Halifax's views. Churchill, among others, noticed this: "I don't think [Halifax] is as far gone as the Prime Minister," he said in February 1939.[34] In the summer of 1939, during the last months before the war, Chamberlain (and behind him Horace Wilson) still encouraged all kinds of dubious and dangerous contacts with some of Hitler's minions; Halifax did not. But once the war began there were no grave clashes among Halifax and Chamberlain and Churchill, all three of them in the cabinet now.

There were, however, differences between Halifax and Churchill on various occasions. During the Reluctant War Halifax was willing to listen (though without committing himself) to various unofficial mediating proposals from all kinds of interlopers. He still had some hope in Goering as a possible successor to Hitler. This did not mean that Halifax was slipping back to appeasement. His principal reason — or at least so he said, on occasion — was to gain time before the full force of the war broke over Britain irrevocably. On 6 May he made an oblique remark in the cabinet, to the effect that "one way to gain time was to delude the Germans by peace talk."[35] The idea of

34. CA 2/343.

35. Unpublished note, left in the Garrowby Album (Halifax family scrapbook), cited in Roberts, *The Holy Fox,* 181. A somewhat curious find, left

"peace talk" stung Churchill to fury. This was high treason, he said. Halifax wrote him immediately: "You are really very unjust to my irresponsible ideas. They may be silly, are certainly dangerous, but are not high treason. I dislike always quarrelling with you! but most of all on 'misunderstood grounds.'" Churchill answered instantly, on the same paper: "Dear Edward. I had a spasm of fear. I am sorry if I offended. It was a vy. deadly thought in this atmosphere of frustration. You cd. not foresee this. Forgive me. W."[36] This was a satisfactory exchange between two old-fashioned gentlemen. The quickly penned phrases and even the handwriting reflect rather well the personal characteristics of their writers. However, as Roberts judiciously puts it, "One has to piece together the evidence for Halifax's relationship with Churchill with care" — and not only because Halifax had "weeded his papers thoroughly." "Many more discussions between Churchill and Halifax took place, particularly in and around cabinet time, than were recorded or recalled."[37]

The inclination to seek compromises, the profound dislike of anything overstated or overwrought, were characteristic of Halifax, not of Churchill. There was more to this than a difference in tactics or perhaps even the difference in their temperaments. Churchill probably understood Halifax better than Halifax understood Churchill, the latter condition having had something to do with Halifax's unwillingness to ponder Churchill's thinking thoroughly. It seems that

---

perhaps by mistake, given Halifax's careful weeding of documents: "Ever the diligent curator of his own reputation, Halifax had afterwards annotated it."

36. It is interesting that the note is on the prime minister's stationery. Did Halifax scribble the note in Chamberlain's office? Or — more probably — was the prime ministerial stationery current in the Cabinet Room?

37. Roberts, *The Holy Fox,* 188.

he thought not only that some of Churchill's proposals or statements were excessive or extreme but that they were superficial. In
short, he was ambivalent about Churchill, distrusting him in some
things, admiring — or at least respecting — his power in others.
There is plenty of evidence for this ambivalence soon after Churchill
became prime minister. On 11 May Halifax congratulated Churchill
in warmest possible terms. (First sentence: "I know how great is the
burden that you have courageously taken upon yourself." Last sentence: "I need not tell you how wholly my thoughts & wishes are
with you in the leadership it now falls to you to give us all. God bless
you always.")[38] Yet on the same day Halifax wrote to his son, an MP,
"I hope Winston won't lead us into anything rash."[39] There are
numerous references critical of Churchill in Halifax's culled diaries
during these days. Did Halifax "simply calculate that he would be in
a more powerful position standing behind the throne than sitting on
it"? Perhaps. He thought that Churchill might not last long. Halifax
wrote in his diary on 11 May: "I have seldom met anybody with
stranger gaps of knowledge, or whose mind worked in greater jerks.
Will it be possible to make it work in orderly fashion? On this much
depends." He added, "Certainly we shall not have gained much in
intellect." On 12 May: "Uneasy about Winston's methods." On
13 May: "Certainly there is no comparison between Winston and
Neville as Chairman." The same day, in a letter: "I don't think WSC
will be a very good PM though I think the country will think he
gives them a fillip." "He's an odd creature." On 14 May: "This makes
me mistrust his judgment more than ever." That day he used the
then-current (here and there) term "gangsters" about Churchill's
new crew: "The gangsters will shortly be in complete control." Yet in

38. CA 20/11.
39. Roberts, *Eminent Churchillians*, 157.

the same diary, on 10 May, about Churchill: "He has acted with great public spirit." On 17 May: "I am much impressed with Winston's courage." Finally, on Friday, 24 May: "I had a talk with Winston before dinner; as always he is full of courage."[40] But he was getting ready to confront him in the War Cabinet.

Halifax still took considerable pleasure from his friendship with the king and queen. On 20 May, walking through the gardens of Buckingham Palace (to the gate of which he had his key from the queen): we "found ourselves enmeshed in a little party on the Lawn, consisting of the King and Queen and the Gloucesters, with whom we had a drink and talk!"[41] On 22 May, Leo Amery, a Churchillite, made a speech at Oxford, about which he recounted: "I thought of saying something by way of warning against the Hitler peace offensive but . . . [the speech was] sent round to Edward [Halifax] who toned it down to something so weak that it almost looked like an invitation to Hitler to offer terms of peace on which we might run out."[42]

◆ ◆ ◆

The time has now come to describe the War Cabinet. After 10 May 1940, the War Cabinet consisted of five men — Churchill, Halifax, and Chamberlain and the two leaders of Labour, Clement Attlee and Arthur Greenwood, who were brought into the coalition, making it a National Government. Sometimes other members of the Outer Cabinet, or high military men, were invited in. Present, too, at times was the cabinet secretary, Sir Edward Bridges; but now and then he

40. Halifax's diaries were written for circulation in his family; many of the above entries are in the diary at York, A.7.8.4. "Gangsters" appears in the Butler Papers; G 11, others in Roberts, *The Holy Fox,* 199. See also Lawlor, *Churchill and the Politics of War,* 35.

41. Halifax Papers, A.7.8.4.

42. Esnouf, "British Government War Aims and Attitudes," 196.

was briefly excluded from the room because of the secrecy of the matters being discussed, which happened during the cabinets of 26 and 27 May.

After the tenth of May, even though he had become prime minister, Churchill chose not yet to move into Downing Street. His rooms were in Admiralty House, where some of the War Cabinet meetings were held, though most of them took place at 10 Downing Street, on the upper floors of which Neville Chamberlain and Mrs. Chamberlain still resided. The Cabinet Room was (and still is) on the ground floor of No. 10, at the end of a long corridor. This was a relatively new arrangement. The larger part of No. 10 Downing Street was built in the late seventeenth century. During the nineteenth century "No. 10" became a password, though not all of the prime ministers chose to live there then. During the twentieth century all of them have done so, except for Churchill during the first months of his prime ministership (and except for Tony Blair now). In 1937 Mrs. Chamberlain, who liked living there, chose to rearrange some of the rooms, mostly on the ground floor.[43] There is a good description of the Cabinet Room in Ian Colvin's *The Chamberlain Cabinet,* a book dealing with 1937–38: "The Cabinet Room, long, narrow and lofty with a table at least twenty-five feet in length, surrounded by sabre-legged and leather-upholstered chairs, had been extended in 1781 with the aid of two Corinthian pillars." There are some nice candlesticks and cut glass on the table, two mantlepiece clocks, and a fine tall-case clock; in the 1930s there were also bookcases and telephones. "A portrait of Sir Robert Walpole by Van Loo hung over the marble fireplace, in front of which the Prime

---

43. Before 1937 Chamberlain lived at 11 Downing Street, the official residence of the chancellor of the exchequer; his own house in Eaton Square he rented to Ribbentrop, then the German ambassador.

" 'The Cabinet Room, long, narrow and lofty with a table at least twenty-five feet in length, surrounded by sabre-legged and leather-upholstered chairs . . .' "

Minister's armchair and inkstand marked the centre of the table. . . . The tall shuttered windows of the Cabinet Room look out over the low garden wall of Number 10, through plane trees on the Horse Guards Parade and St. James's Park." Outside the red baize door, "in the ante-room, brass-framed labels indicated where each Minister might hang his hat."[44]

It would seem, at first sight, that Churchill had a comfortable majority in the War Cabinet, not to speak of the Outer one: even if

44. Colvin, *The Chamberlain Cabinet* 18, 21.

Chamberlain and Halifax were to oppose him, the two Labour ministers would support him, three to two, at worst. This was so, but it only went so far. Attlee and Greenwood were newcomers in the cabinet, and their experience in military and world affairs was limited; besides, they represented a party that was very much of a minority in Parliament. In May 1940 they listened rather than spoke (especially Attlee) in the War Cabinet. A real break between Churchill and the two eminent Conservatives would have been disastrous. Had Halifax or Chamberlain or both resigned, there would have been a national crisis, immediately reverberating in Parliament, and Churchill's position would have been gravely damaged, perhaps even untenable.

On Friday, 24 May, the War Cabinet met at 11:30 A.M. Most of the discussion involved Calais, about which Churchill talked at some length. It appears that he was not yet informed about Hitler's halt order. There was, for the first time, mention of Dunkirk: "Considerable numbers of French troops were in Dunkirk, but no English troops had as yet been sent there, with the exception of certain small units sent back to this area from the B.E.F. The port was functioning quite well."[45] Then Halifax brought up the Belgian crisis: there was more discussion about whether preparations should be made for King Leopold III and his family to depart for England, as the queen of Holland and her entourage had done twelve days earlier. Halifax said yes, Churchill, not yet. But there was no real conflict between them on this point.

Neither Churchill nor Halifax knew of a significant development in Washington that day, 24 May. Since the beginning of the war Churchill had had a secret correspondence with President Roosevelt. Halifax knew this and approved it. But—and this is important—

45. CAB 65/7.

as late as mid-May 1940 Roosevelt was not yet confident about the worth of Churchill's leadership. He had received differing reports about Churchill's character, not all of them positive.[46] There was, too, his ambassador in London, Joseph Kennedy, who, as we have seen, hated Churchill and thought that England had no chance of (or reason for) resisting Germany. Roosevelt had begun to be aware of Kennedy's defeatist tendencies; so had Halifax. But more important was the startling nature of the message that Churchill had composed and sent to Roosevelt on 15 May. This was the first revelation of Churchill looking ahead into the abyss, of his recognition that he might be cast aside if Britain were compelled to sue for peace. (Note how early — this is the afternoon of 15 May — Churchill envisages the possibility of France falling.) "As you are no doubt aware, the scene has darkened swiftly," he wrote. "If necessary, we shall continue the war alone and we are not afraid of that. But I trust you realise, Mr President, that the voice and the force of a United States may count for nothing if they are withheld too long. You may have a completely subjugated, Nazified Europe established with astonish-

46. Sumner Welles in March, after he had visited London: Churchill was unsteady, drinking too much. Adolf Berle, assistant secretary of state: Churchill may be too old and "tired." On 11 May Churchill was discussed at the White House. Harold Ickes, secretary of the interior: "Apparently Churchill is very unreliable under the influence of drink." Roosevelt said that he "supposed Churchill was the best man England had." Frances Perkins, secretary of labor: Roosevelt was "uncertain" about Churchill, asking his cabinet members "what kind of man" Churchill really was. Ickes: Churchill was "too old." Add to this the view of Mrs. Roosevelt, who thought that Churchill was "reactionary"; she had gone so far as to ask a friend to impress that upon her husband (Lukacs, *The Duel,* 73). About the early Churchill-Roosevelt relationship, ibid., 72–74.

ing swiftness, *and the weight may be more than we can bear.*" The italics are mine.

Roosevelt answered Churchill's message twelve hours after its receipt. His tone was friendly, but he did not promise much. Two days later Churchill acknowledged Roosevelt's response in a short letter of five sentences. "We are determined to persevere to the very end whatever the result of the great battle raging in France may be. . . . But if American assistance is to play any part it must be available soon." Another two days later, on the twenty-first, Churchill drafted another letter. He hesitated whether to send it. In the end he did. He felt compelled to impress upon Roosevelt the awful prospect of what might happen. His government might go down in battle, "but in no conceivable circumstances we will consent to surrender." But:

> If members of the present administration were finished and others came in to parley amid the ruins, you must not be blind to the fact that the sole remaining bargaining counter with Germany would be the fleet, and if this country was left by the United States to its fate no one would have the right to blame those then responsible if they made the best terms they could for the surviving inhabitants. Excuse me, Mr President, putting this nightmare bluntly. Evidently I could not answer for my successors who in utter despair and helplessness might well have to accommodate themselves to the German will.

Churchill ended, "However there is happily no need at present to dwell upon such ideas."

Happily no need? Perhaps the prospect of such ideas was unthinkable, but the unthinkable must sometimes be thought about, and the time had come to give it at least some thought. Roosevelt and others in Washington did not realize this fully or even adequately. Roosevelt's trust in and friendship with Churchill were not yet strong enough. There was still a distance between their minds. For almost another month no important messages would pass between them.

Meanwhile a dangerous fracas broke to the surface in London. A member of the American embassy there, the code clerk Tyler Kent, was a convinced isolationist. Not unlike some American isolationists and at least some Republicans, his extreme dislike of Franklin Roosevelt went hand in hand with his anti-Communism and pro-German worldview. He had taken hundreds of classified documents, including secret messages from Churchill to Roosevelt and vice versa, from the American embassy and hoarded them in his home near Baker Street. He passed some of these to a handful of people, mostly women who hated Churchill and who were German sympathizers, some of the papers then going on to a few British Fascists and even to Italian agents. On 20 May British security police broke into the room of this Baker Street Irregular. Then his diplomatic immunity was waived. He was sentenced to seven years in prison. (At the end of the war he was released and returned to the United States.) It is interesting to note that there was nothing unconstitutional in the contents of the Churchill-Roosevelt correspondence. It was fortunate that Roosevelt's ambassador Kennedy, whose political preferences were similar to Kent's, chose to wash his hands of Kent and would not insist on his immunity. Kennedy the politician chose not to break with Roosevelt before the 1940 election campaign; he did not think that this was the right occasion or the right time to cause open trouble for Roosevelt.[47]

47. These two pages, including the passages from Churchill's messages, from ibid., 75–77.

On 23 May Churchill informed the War Cabinet that the prime ministers of Australia and New Zealand had sent a secret and urgent telegram suggesting that in view of the gravity of the situation, the Dominion governments should severally address appeals to President Roosevelt for the release of every available aircraft and that they should also appeal for American volunteer pilots. Churchill's reply was that he "should not recommend a public appeal at this moment, for it would give the President an impression of weakness."[48] That evening Kennedy met with Halifax. Kennedy was utterly pessimistic about England's chances and volubly critical of Churchill. He sent a message to Roosevelt in the same vein. Roosevelt was inclined to listen to his friend William C. Bullitt, the American ambassador to France, who had already suggested (on 16 May) that there was the possibility not only of a French but of an eventual British surrender, in which event the British ought to move their fleet to Canada.

This was in accord with Roosevelt's views. He had begun to realize the swiftness and the gravity of events. Even before his unprecedented attempt at a third term of office, he was beginning to think, somewhat as the British on 10 May had, of a national coalition government. He had talked to his 1936 presidential opponent, Alfred Landon, about this, though as yet without results. Now, on the morning of 24 May, he contacted the prime minister of Canada, Mackenzie King, asking him to send a secret representative to Washington to discuss "certain possible eventualities which could not possibly be mentioned aloud." On the telephone King was referred to as Mr. Kick, Roosevelt as Mr. Roberts. King thought that the United States was "trying to save itself at the expense of Britain" and told Roosevelt that he should talk about that to Churchill directly.

48. CAB 65/7. Churchill's answer to the Australian prime minister appears in Gilbert, *The Churchill War Papers, Companion Volume 2,* 119.

Roosevelt's idea (and request) was that Canada and the Dominions should press Churchill to send the British fleet across the Atlantic, the sooner the better — that is, before Hitler's peace terms could include the surrender of the fleet. Roosevelt added that Churchill should not be told of the American origin of that proposal. Thus Roosevelt himself had come to realize that Britain might have to sue for peace — that is, surrender. Also, he did not quite — yet — trust Churchill.

Of this Churchill — and Halifax — were unaware.

♦ ♦ ♦

So, too, were the people of Britain largely unaware of the immediacy of the dangers that faced them. This relative unawareness was reflected in the press. This is significant, since even during the war there was considerable freedom of the press in Britain. When it came to secret or sensitive matters the government would rely much less on peremptory state censorship than on the habitual self-censorship of the newspapers' editors and of their reporters. The historian who wishes to reconstruct from the British newspapers the public opinion of the period may find plentiful illustrations of daily life from various small news items, programs, advertisements, and so on, as the layout and the contents and the very character of British newspapers hardly differed from their makeup before the war; however, as purveyors of the kind of news that was otherwise not available, say, on the radio, the newspapers told little. Only here and there can we find in the newspapers items that reflect expressions or tendencies of public opinion not recorded elsewhere. We shall come to one or two of these in a moment.

Meanwhile, the newspapers' reportage and comment on the grave and dramatic military events in France and Belgium were generally wanting. About this there was no great difference between the more detailed and highbrow "class" newspapers such as the *Times* or the

Daily Telegraph on the one hand and the popular newspapers on the other. On 24 May the editorial in the *Evening Standard* was perhaps unusual because of its somber warning to prepare for the worst: "First let us have no ostrichism in our preparations against an invasion of this island. There are still some who scorn the idea. Can Hitler succeed where Napoleon failed? No, they say, the Channel is impregnable, just as others told us some weeks ago that the Meuse was impregnable. We would do better to prepare for the worst." The editorial of the *News Chronicle* was sober: "In his brief statement on the war situation yesterday the Prime Minister made it clear that the tide of German penetration into Belgium and Northern France has not yet been stemmed." Yet it also printed a headline, "French Troops at Suburbs of Amiens," which was, unfortunately, far from the truth. In the same number the renowned military expert Liddell Hart wrote that bombing power now made it difficult, if not impossible, "to maintain a bridgehead" on a Channel port (fortunately he was to be proved wrong, about Dunkirk at least). A G. G. S. Salusbury, war correspondent of the *Daily Herald,* was very wrong: "Britain and France are unbeaten. The main French armies, the main British armies, have not yet been seriously engaged." The *Manchester Guardian* praised the French "Aged Commanders," Weygand and Pétain: they had their "coevals in years among the great figures of history." Weygand was seventy-three, but the Doge Enrico Dandolo of Venice had led his army into Constantinople when he was ninety-five. Marshal Pétain was eighty-four, but then Gladstone (still hero of the liberal *Manchester Guardian*) was still prime minister at eighty-four, and "if (as M. Reynaud tells us) Marshal Pétain is to stay in office until victory had been won he may outlast Gladstone's record." Yet the *Manchester Guardian*'s editorial that day was good: "Vigilance. German arms roll nearer to us every day. . . . Morale is not preserved by closing the eyes. Too much had been lost in this war already by refusals to believe that certain things could happen." There is a prewar, if not Edwardian, touch in the programs announced by the Manchester theaters for the week following 24 May: *The Chocolate Soldier* in the Opera House. *Gaietés de Montmartre* in the Gaiety Theatre. (In the two large movie theaters, *The Hunchback of Notre Dame* and *Destry Rides Again,* with Marlene Dietrich.) The main article in the *Daily Telegraph* was written by J. B. Firth, a historian and biographer of Cromwell. Its tone was Churchillian: "Now is the time for the British people to show the stuff of which they are made and the heights to which they can soar. . . . Hitler's peace propaganda before the war was directly designed to spread terror. . . . Duty calls us to close ranks at home against the slightest sign of national disunity." Was this whistling in the dark? Perhaps not. The "London News and Comment" section of the *Scotsman* declared on 24 May, "The confidence of the Londoner remains unshaken by the news from France, even though it is graver."[49]

Three items appearing in most of the newspapers on 24 May may have some significance. One was the front-page treatment, and

49. "During the last war Shakespeare was played continuously at the Old Vic, and it is again the intention of that theatre to keep the door open. . . . Sadlers' Wells Ballet lost music, scenery and dresses in Holland a fortnight ago, and has had to revise its repertory. Its London season will open on 4 June." (The *Times,* 24 May, praised Richard Tauber's performance of Schumann songs and Joseph Weingarten's Beethoven piano concert: "At the end the audience could feel that they had listened to a serious interpretation of one of Beethoven's noblest works.") An entire page (5) of the *Scotsman* was devoted to the General Assembly of the Church of Scotland, Home and Foreign Missions Day: "Praying about peace, advocating prayers for victory, declared the Rev. Ewan Maclean, 'we could have peace tomorrow—the *Pax Germanica.*'"

unanimous approval, of the government's decision to arrest Oswald Mosley and his wife, together with the Germanophile Captain Ramsay, member of Parliament, and other Fascists (more than one thousand of them). Other, less agreeable evidence of superpatriotism were numerous letters to editors and even some articles protesting against the presence and the free movements of German refugees (those writing were either unaware of or indifferent to the condition that most of these refugees were anti-Nazis and Jews).[50] Suspicion of aliens showed up in many newspapers: in the *News Chronicle* there were a number of letters critical of refugees ("Where does their money come from?"). On the same page the *News Chronicle* reported that the Dagenham Girl Pipers had applied "for permission to form a defence rifle corps."

One interesting sign — interesting mostly because of its long-range significance — was the attention devoted in the newspapers to relations with Russia: a kind of anxious looking around for eventual allies. This accorded, by and large, with the intention of the government — of Halifax as well as of Churchill — to improve these relations, to send Sir Stafford Cripps on another mission to Moscow, as early as 18 May. On the twenty-fourth the *News Chronicle* quoted R. A. Butler: "We are taking immediate steps to improve our relations with the Soviets." "Our London Correspondent" of the *Manchester Guardian* had a telephone interview with G. B. Shaw, who praised both Stalin and the British resolution to fight to the bitter end: "An understanding with him is vital." That understanding

---

50. The lead article in the *Daily Mail,* 24 May, was about the fifth column: "There has been swift action on the home front. The Fifth Column in Britain are beginning to totter. Yesterday the authorities struck. The peril of inward rot is at least obvious to everyone. Holland fell in five days because no man could trust his neighbour." (That is not why Holland fell.)

would not come for a long time, although not for a lack of British willingness for it. When on 22 June 1941 Hitler's invasion of the Soviet Union brought about a de facto alliance between Britain and Russia, there followed a wave of Russophilia in Britain, partly of course because of the relief that people felt not only about the course of the war but also about the slackening of the German bombing of Britain. Yet such inclinations, including illusions about Russia, had their forerunners in May 1940, and not only among leftist intellectuals or elements of the British working class.

The Mass-Observation reports recorded, as usual, reactions and expressions that were more varied than what appeared in the press. The summary "Morale Today" of 24 May reported little change, "though perhaps a slight increase in anxiety and a slight decrease in optimism. There is a general recognition of the seriousness of the situation, but still extremely little idea that this could be more than a temporary setback or could lead to an attempt to invade ourselves" [*sic*]. The general impression is of an uneasy fluctuation of moods: "It cannot be good for people's nerves to pin so much on the small incidents of each day, to give a great gasp of relief and happiness at a headline about Arras, to be plunged into temporary gloom by bad news about Boulogne." "A new feature today is the great increase and sometimes intense violence of criticism against the French."[51] "All these remarks apply particularly to the upper and middle classes, and to women." Yet in the same report there is an account of a conversation among middle-aged trade unionists: "Do you know, our women went round canvassing for the Housewives Union and some of them, especially some of the younger housewives they talked to — have got to the stage where they would more or less

51. FR 134. Typical comments: "What's the use of France? Or if they have an army what do they do with it?"

welcome Hitler here. They say it couldn't be worse, and they'd at least have their husbands back." "That's right. . . . They say it can't be worse, so what's the good of fighting? I can see that if the morale goes on the decline so steep as it is at the moment, there won't be much resistance to him, when he does come."[52]

But that was not typical. More typical was the universal approval for the arrest of Mosley. And perhaps the words of "Nella," an M-O reporter in Bolton who wrote 2 million words during the war, published in a book forty years later. On 11 May she wrote: "If I had to spend my whole life with a man, I'd choose Chamberlain, but I think I would sooner have Mr Churchill if there was a storm and I was shipwrecked."[53] One interesting condition in both the M-O and the Ministry of Information reports and diaries is the almost entire absence of comments about Halifax. People were indifferent, even ignorant, about him. There is a single report of the words of one man on 11 May: "Halifax wants to be made Archbishop of Canterbury. He doesn't want to be in the Cabinet."

52. FR 134, 24 May, pp. 3, iii.
53. *Nella's Last War.*

CHAPTER THREE

Saturday, 25 May

*An English weekend. – The French: Weygand and Pétain. – Halifax
and the Italian ambassador. – Churchill and the Defence Committee. –
"Depression is quite definitely up."*

Over most of Europe and England the weather was beautiful in
May 1940 — relentless sunshine pouring over the land, the calmest of
seas (which was to be a blessing for the British once the sea haul
from Dunkirk back to Dover began). None of the great capital cities
of the warring nations had, as yet, the experience of bombs raining
down upon them. Everyday life went on in London, as it went on in
Berlin and Paris, although in London, unlike in Paris or Berlin,
sandbagged small barricades with armed sentries went up before
some of the principal government buildings. Still there was a special
quality of the calmness of London on a Saturday, because of the
English weekend habit. A vignette of 25 May, Saturday, from Evelyn
Waugh's wartime diary: "This morning, just as the battalion had
decided that its training was so deficient that we must break up into

cadres, the Brigadier, having boasted that we would have held Boulogne, reported us as trained and ready for service. Cadre training will continue. The major put in charge has eluded all responsibility and left me in charge of the NCO's cadre. . . . At midday Saturday, Laura and I set off for an idyllic weekend at Alton in the Swan Hotel. A charming town not only devoid of military but full of personable young civilians of military age. A hotel full of foliage plants and massive, elaborate furniture. We went to church, read P. G. Wodehouse (who has been lost along the Channel ports),[1] watched old men in panama hats play bowl, and forgot the war."[2]

The "London News and Comment" column of the *Scotsman* reported on 25 May: "During these days of anxiety, London life proceeds with every outward appearance of normality. On the surface, at least, it is difficult to find signs comparable with the uneasiness which prevailed in the first few days of September when the realities of war were yet to come." West End shopping streets were "far from deserted." The list of entertainments in the newspapers was long and

---

1. P. G. Wodehouse and his wife were in Le Touquet when the Germans arrived. The Germans treated them (as they also treated other English residents) with considerable courtesy. Wodehouse was favorably impressed with the Germans' behavior and let them persuade him to give a talk, in English, on the German radio. His broadcast was mildly humorous and mild in sentiment. Reading the broadcast today, one can find little or nothing objectionable in it, though its attribution to Wodehouse's naïveté is perhaps too simplistic. Subsequently he was fiercely attacked in Britain, where some accused him of treachery. That was a malevolent exaggeration. After the liberation of Paris, Malcolm Muggeridge, George Orwell, and others, including Waugh, tried their best to rehabilitate Wodehouse. This eventually happened, though Wodehouse, having translated himself to America, never returned to England.

2. *Diaries of Evelyn Waugh,* 470.

varied.[3] Both the *Daily Mail* and the *Daily Express* printed half pages of holiday advertisements for places on the southern coast of England.[4] The *Manchester Guardian* advertised a vacation in Paris: "STAY IN PARIS near the Opera and the Grands Boulevards. Ambassador, 16, Boulevard Haussmann. Room (running water and private w.c.) from 55 Frs. Special rates for members of Allied forces."

Allied forces notwithstanding, there was a prewar tone and touch to this and other advertisements of the daily newspapers. There was no prewar tone in the deliberations of the highest council of the French who met that Saturday evening. It was postwar rather than prewar: postwar in the sense that the supreme commander of the French army was proposing an ending of the war, that is, surrender, to Hitler.

◆ ◆ ◆

There were many in France — many more than in England — who did not have their hearts in the war. There were such people in the government and among the representatives elected to the Chambers. There were at least three reasons for their state of mind, reasons on different levels, involving also people with different inclinations. Perhaps instead of "reasons" we should say "elements." The overwhelming element was the memory of the last war, in which France had lost 1.4 million men. The French population now was aged, especially when compared to those of Germany and Italy.

---

3. The *Daily Herald* cites Miss Doreen Porcheron, "one of the two West End chorus girls who undertook to fight 'vulgar nudity' on the stage."

4. The *Daily Mail*, 25 May: "Ryde, Isle of Wight: 30 minutes' pleasant crossing over sheltered waters bring you to this Peaceful, Carefree, Holidayland!" (Only one or two days later the Isle of Wight steamers left for Dover and then to Dunkirk.) The *Daily Express*, 25 May: "Ramsgate: Your Place in the Sun for Holidays as Usual!" Worthing: "Your Wartime Choice!"

There were almost three times as many Germans and Italians of military age as there were Frenchmen. Yet defeatism was not widespread among the French people, not even after the Black Fortnight of May 1940. The civilian population showed a remarkable degree of quiet discipline, behaving better than did some of the soldiers, especially those of the Ninth Army at the Meuse. That would change once the German onslaught approached French towns and villages. Then there would follow an enormous wave of mass flight and panic, but not much of that had occurred, as yet, in May.

The French politicians were divided. Many of them thought — and muttered, rather than said openly — that France should not have gone to war in September 1939. Again, as in so many other countries, the division was not so much between Right and Left as between two Rights: between those who thought that this war was a mistake and others who thought that France, because of her traditions and honor, had no other choice. Did the former consider that if France were to acquiesce in the German (and Italian) domination of all of Europe, except perhaps for the few democracies on the western edge of the Continent, this would reduce France to the state of a Belgium or a Holland, to a timorous neutrality, hardly able — and unwilling — to oppose almost anything that Hitler or Mussolini would demand? Even after nearly sixty years we cannot answer this question, because the antiwar politicians had not put this question to themselves. For many of them, their motives were ideological as much as political. They thought that France would be better off seeking an accommodation with Mussolini than becoming dependent on England. Anglophobia, rather than pro-Fascism, was the common denominator of these preferences, ideas, and sentiments, yet in many cases it included an ideological element. They were convinced not only that the British were hypocritical and selfish but that their system and their view of the world were old and probably useless, which was not the case with the new order of Mussolini or, alas, of Hitler either.

The events of the Black Fortnight activated these sentiments. Those who held them blamed not the wretched performance of some of their own army but the British. The British and the Anglophile politicians in Paris, this reasoning went, had gotten France into this war. After that the British sent but a few divisions and a few squadrons of airplanes to France, and now they were retreating to the Channel ports, abandoning the French. They were also false; they were not telling the French what they were doing. There was some reason to arrive at such conclusions. We have seen that the British, including Churchill, were considering withdrawal to the ports and evacuation to England days before the twenty-fifth of May. The previous night Reynaud had telegraphed to Churchill that the British army "was no longer conforming to General Weygand's plan and has withdrawn toward the Channel ports." Churchill had answered, "We have every reason to believe that Gort is still persevering in his southward move." This was not so. Two British divisions were withdrawing from Arras. Churchill knew that the "Weygand plan," the joint Franco-British counterattack, amounted to nothing: "Nothing in the movement of the B.E.F. of which we are aware can be any excuse for the abandonment of the strong pressure of your northward move across the Somme, which we trust will develop."[5] There was no such pressure, strong or weak, and Churchill must have known that develop it would not. There was a War Cabinet at 11:30. Churchill informed his colleagues of his exchange with Reynaud, adding: "No doubt the action taken had been forced on Lord Gort by the position in which he had found himself. Never-

5. CA 20/14; also in Gilbert, *Companion Volume,* 140.

theless, he should at once have informed us of the action which he had taken, and the French had grounds for complaint. But this was no time for recriminations."[6]

General Weygand and Marshal Pétain thought that the time had come for recriminations — and then some. Weygand was the newly appointed commander-in-chief, Pétain a national hero from the First World War whom Reynaud had appointed as his vice premier but three days before. They distrusted the British, and they were opposed to the Anglo-French alliance from the beginning. There were many indications of this, especially on the part of Pétain, who knew that he had his partisans. The previous day Pierre Laval, after 1935 a convinced Anglophobe, spoke to an Italian diplomat in Paris, whose report to Rome is telling: "Laval thinks that more than ever it has become indispensable and urgent to establish contact with Rome." It is "the only way to talk with Hitler. The present government will not do that. A Pétain-Laval government must come."[7]

At seven in the evening of 25 May the highest council, the Comité de Guerre, convened in Paris. Present were the president of the Republic, Albert Lebrun; Premier Reynaud; Pétain; Weygand; two other ministers; two other generals; and the secretary of the Comité de Guerre, a Pétain follower. Weygand began with a long account. The military situation, he said, was impossible and hopeless. "We have to fight one against three." "We will be smashed." What remains, then, is that "each portion of the army must fight until exhausted, to save the honor of the country." Then came Weygand's conclusion: "France had committed the immense mistake to enter

6. CAB 65/7.

7. Giobbe (Paris) in *Documenti diplomatici italiani,* 1939–43, series 9, vol. 4, 439.

into the war without the material or the military doctrine that were needed. It is probable that [France] will have to pay dearly for this criminal thoughtlessness."

Then the president of the Republic, Lebrun, spoke: "We are committed not to sign a separate peace." (In March the French and British governments made such a reciprocal commitment.) "Still — if Germany offers us conditions that are relatively advantageous, we must examine them closely and with calm heads."[8] Weygand agreed. Reynaud intervened: "If we were presented with a peace offer, France, in any case, must tell the British. . . . We are bound by a formal commitment." Now Pétain: "I question whether there is a complete reciprocity with the British. . . . Actually they have given only two divisions while eighty French divisions are still fighting." Reynaud considered, "An exchange of views with England may be justified, if only because one may ask them whether they would be ready to agree to important sacrifices to prevent Italy from entering the war." There was a brave countermove by the minister of the navy, Campinchi: "The loyalty of France must not be risked; a peace treaty must never be signed by France without a previous agreement with England. [I am] not entirely in agreement with Marshal Pétain when the Marshal compares the military contribution of the two nations. . . . If this government had given its word to England, perhaps another government might feel less bound to the signing of

---

8. As a matter of fact the Swedish minister to France, Nordling, brought an indirect message from Goering to Reynaud on 19 May. (Nordling was in Stockholm on 10 May and saw Goering in Berlin on the fifteenth, arriving in Paris on the seventeenth.) On 26 May Goering met with another Swede, Dahlerus, a fervent partisan of an accommodation between Britain and Germany; at that time, however, their talks concerned the future of northern Norway and Narvik.

a peace treaty without the former agreement with England." But "being unfortunate is one thing; being disloyal another. It is urgent now to talk to the English."

There was another verbal skirmish between Campinchi and Weygand. Reynaud then declared that he would go to London the next day to explain "clearly the situation to the English: the inequality of fighting with one against four; but that nonetheless the French government was ready to continue the struggle even if it would be fighting for one's honor." He would ask the English what would happen if Paris were to fall. Their response might be, "You are bound by your signature; you must fight even when hopeless." But Weygand had the last word. The total destruction of the French armed forces, fighting to the end only to save their honor? "We must preserve the instruments of order. What troubles would result if the last organized force, that is the Army, is destroyed?" "The English must be sounded on all these questions."[9] Reynaud consented. The entire meeting took two and a half hours.

◆ ◆ ◆

A few hours before this momentous gathering of the French leaders in Paris (the essence of which the British remained unaware), Lord Halifax chose to make an attempt of his own. He asked the Italian ambassador, Giuseppe Bastianini, to meet him that afternoon. This was somewhat unusual since it occurred on the weekend, which many people in Britain, among them foreign ambassadors and Halifax himself, still observed. The tone of their conversation, including Halifax's careful and sober language, was of course very different from what Weygand and Pétain were saying in

9. The minutes are reproduced in François Delpla, *Les Papiers secrets du général Doumenc,* Annexe 6: "Comité de Guerre du samedi 25 mai 1940," 504–9.

the depressive and agitated climate of the French Council of War. Yet their purposes were not entirely different: to prevent Italy from entering the war, with concessions, if necessary — and, concealed behind his matter, the suggestion that Mussolini might be instrumental in bringing about a "general European settlement."

We must, at this point, consider the — in retrospect, surprising — importance of Italy among the European, indeed world powers in the 1930s. Mussolini's prestige was such that when, in 1935–36, he decided to move Italy from a possibly anti-German coalition to the German side, this weighed much more in the European balance of power than the contemporary commitment (1934–35) of Stalin's Soviet Union to enter into a military alliance with France and thus join the anti-Hitler front. With the Italian conquest of Abyssinia and then of Albania, Bismarck's once-acid comment to the effect that Italy had a good appetite but poor teeth was largely forgotten. Added to this was the impression that Mussolini had been principally instrumental, prevailing with Hitler in bringing about the Munich conference in September 1938, one step away from the abyss of war. Within France, admiration for Mussolini had a definite ideological element; within Britain, less so. Yet it was Chamberlain's stubborn wish to curry favor with Mussolini that precipitated Anthony Eden's resignation and Halifax's assumption of the foreign secretaryship in February 1938 (Churchill's sleepless night). This was preceded by joint intrigues between Italian agents and some of Chamberlain's people (including Sir Joseph Ball, a minor version of Horace Wilson), including the tapping of telephone conversations. In January 1939 Chamberlain and Halifax visited Rome, without much result. In May 1939 Italy signed a "Steel Pact" with Germany. In September 1939 Mussolini's decision of "non-belligerence," meaning that Italy would not yet enter the war, brought relief to London and Paris. But then Mussolini began to range himself on

Hitler's side more and more unconditionally. As late as April 1940 Halifax still thought that Mussolini might not do so.[10] But there were fewer and fewer reasons for the British to doubt that Mussolini would enter the war, sooner rather than later.

Then came the triumphant march of the Germans across northern France. On 16 May Churchill wrote an impressive letter to Mussolini: "I beg you to believe that it is in no spirit of weakness or of fear that I make this solemn appeal which will remain on record. Down the ages above all other calls came the cry that the joint heirs of Latin and Christian civilization must not be ranged against one another in mortal strife." Two days later came Mussolini's answer: "If it was to honour your signature that your Government declared war on Germany, you will understand that the same sense of honour and of respect for engagements assumed in the Italian-German Treaty guided Italian policy today and tomorrow in the face of any event whatsoever." Churchill: "The response was hard. It had at least the merit of candour."[11]

This exchange was not communicated to the Italian ambassador in London. Bastianini, though an early Fascist, was neither an Anglophobe nor a committed Germanophile. It is not possible to ascertain whether the initiative leading to his talk with Halifax came from him or from Halifax's side: probably the latter.[12] Around 20 May Bastianini had met with Lord Phillimore, who reported their conversation to Butler, who was enthusiastic: "Hitler would

10. On 6 April 1940: "I still adhere to my view that [Musso] is going to bark more than bite" (Halifax Papers, A.7.8.3). Halifax was wrong.

11. Churchill, *Their Finest Hour,* 122.

12. It is perhaps noteworthy that in Bastianini's autobiographical essays, *Uomini, cose, fatti: Memorie d'un ambasciatore,* there is nothing about Halifax and May 1940.

listen to [Mussolini] and him alone, even now."[13] Halifax did not tell Churchill this, but he thought it prudent to inform the War Cabinet on 25 May that "at the invitation of a third party a meeting had taken place between Sir Robert Vansittart and a member of the staff of the Italian Embassy." This man (whose name was Paresci) said that "if His Majesty's Government saw their way to make an approach to the Italian Government, with a view to exploring the possibilities of a friendly settlement, there need be no fear of their meeting with a rebuff." Halifax was treading gingerly. "After consulting with the Prime Minister, the Foreign Secretary had been authorized to pursue the matter further." There would be a second meeting between Vansittart and the Italian. "Very likely nothing might come of all this. Nevertheless, even if the result were merely to gain time, it would be valuable." Churchill said that he did not object to the meeting but cautioned that "it must not, of course, be accompanied by any publicity, since that would amount to a confession of weakness."[14]

Halifax met Bastianini that afternoon. He reported their conversation in considerable detail: "It was quite true that we had intended to make an approach, in appropriate form, to certain political questions . . . and in any such approach we should have wished to make plain our desire that Italy should naturally take her proper place at a peace conference by the side of the belligerents. . . . If and when we should receive an indication that our approach might be received with due consideration, we should be prepared to carry the matter

13. Roberts, *The Holy Fox,* 212.

14. CAB 65/7. WM 138 (40). Halifax may have had his reasons for bringing up Vansittart (who could never be accused of being pro-appeasement), but not Butler.

further and deal with it in greater detail. . . . [It] might serve to open the way to the treatment of other questions, always provided that we could approach these questions on the basis of the frankest recognition of the rights and necessities of both parties." Bastianini answered that he would of course immediately pass on what Halifax had said to his government, adding, however, that it had always been Mussolini's view that "the settlement of problems between Italy and any other country should be part of a general European settlement." Bastianini asked Halifax "whether he might inform his Government that His Majesty's Government considered it opportune now to examine the question at issue between our two countries within the larger framework of a European settlement."[15]

Halifax said that he "had always thought, if any discussions were to be held with a view of solving European questions and building a peaceful Europe, that matters which caused anxiety to Italy must certainly be discussed as part of the general European settlement." Now Bastianini moved a bit forward. "He would like to know whether His Majesty's Government would consider it possible to discuss general questions involving not only Great Britain and Italy, but other countries." He meant Germany, of course. "On my saying [Halifax] that it was difficult to visualize such wide discussions while the war was still proceeding," the ambassador replied that, "once such a discussion were begun, war would be pointless." Mussolini, said Bastianini, was concerned to build a settlement "that

15. Did he? His version of the conversation with Halifax (see below) was not telegraphed to Rome until twenty-four hours later (and received in Rome at 5:20 A.M. on 27 May). Even given the weekend and the time necessary for encrypting it, this seems slow. In the margin of the dispatch there is Mussolini's signature: he read it.

would not merely be an armistice but would protect European peace for the century." Halifax said, "The purpose of His Majesty's Government was the same, and they would never be unwilling to consider any proposal made with authority that gave promise of the establishment of a secure and peaceful Europe." To this Bastianini "warmly agreed": "He would like to be able to inform Signor Mussolini that His Majesty's Government did not exclude the possibility of some discussion of the wider problems of Europe in the event of the opportunity arising." "This I told [Bastianini] he could certainly do."[16]

This is Halifax's carefully worded précis of his talk with the Italian ambassador. Bastianini's record of their conversation is not very different, except that in his version, unlike Halifax's, Germany, as such, was mentioned. According to Bastianini, Halifax, among other matters, "fully recognized the special relationship of Italy with Germany," and that in accord with Bastianini's personal opinion, "the problem of the Italian-British relationship cannot be considered, given the actual situation and the special Italian-German relationship, except in the greater and more enduring framework of a just and enduring European settlement."[17]

There is nothing about this significant conversation (indeed, not a single mention of Bastianini) in Halifax's bland memoirs or, perhaps more significantly, in his diaries. According to Roberts, Halifax's biographer: "In September 1948 Lord Ismay persuaded Churchill to excise a passage in Volume Two of his *War Memoirs,* which dealt with the Bastianini affair and read, 'The Foreign Secretary showed himself willing to go a long way.' Churchill magnanimously

16. Annex to CAB 66/7. The text is Halifax's dispatch to Sir Percy Loraine, British ambassador in Rome, 212 FO 800/319/70.

17. *Documenti diplomatici italiani, 1939–1943,* series 9, vol. 4, 462–63.

went so far as to alter the passage." In reality, Churchill omitted the entire matter. "Halifax showed little thanks."[18]

◆ ◆ ◆

That same afternoon, 25 May, Hitler dictated an unusually verbose letter to Mussolini. Hitler knew that Mussolini had decided to enter the war, probably within the next fortnight, which is why it does not behoove us to analyze this long epistle in detail, except perhaps for one matter: Hitler, in passing, wrote about the temporary halt of the German spearheads before Dunkirk (adding that the corrupt press of the Western Powers drew false conclusions from that, which was not the case), assuring Mussolini that it would last not more than two days. This was so: he lifted the halt order the next day.

Churchill's Saturday schedule was unusually full but perhaps not extraordinary. There was a cabinet meeting at 11:30. The Attlees

18. Roberts, *The Holy Fox,* 229; Ismay Papers, CA 11/3/100/2. Halifax often criticized Churchill's war memoirs privately. Roberts's analysis of the Halifax-Bastianini conversation is worth considering: "There were two totally different Allied plans for action with regard to Italy that were over the next three days to be constantly mixed up and confused with one another. To make matters worse, some politicians, including Halifax, later pretended to be referring to one when it was in fact the other, and after the war they denied the existence of one of the plans altogether. The first was the plan to bribe Mussolini to stay out of the war and the second a scheme to attempt to persuade him to intercede with Hitler to procure reasonable terms for a permanent cease-fire. The two were, of course, mutually contradictory: the first being designed to facilitate the more successful waging of the very war which the second intended to bring to an end" (ibid., 213). Not necessarily: the hope for Mussolini as peacemaker could encompass both, and the two plans did not seem contradictory to either Halifax or Bastianini at the time.

came for lunch in Admiralty House. At 5:30 he met the Defence Committee in Downing Street, where the discussion mostly concerned the situation in Flanders and the Belgians.[19] The British did not know what the king of Belgium, Leopold III, had said to three of his ministers that day: "The cause of the Allies is lost. . . . No doubt England will continue the war, not on the Continent, but on the seas and in the colonies, but Belgium can play no part in it. Her role is terminated. . . . There is no reason for us to continue the war on the side of the Allies." (He also said that Queen Wilhelmina of Holland ought not to stay in Britain.)[20]

General Ismay sent a paper to Churchill about the prospect of a German intervention in Ireland, which he doubted.[21] At 8:30 "Lord Beaverbrook, Prof. Lindemann, Mr Bracken to dinner." Churchill was still full of energy. Immediately after dinner, at 10:00 P.M., there was a second Defence Committee meeting in his quarters in Admiralty House. It was now evident that there was no chance for a southward move of some of the BEF, coordinated with the French. "Having regard to the practical certainty that no effective French offensive was likely to be launched from south of the Somme for some considerable time, the view was generally expressed that an immediate march to the coast was the right course." (They did not know that Gort had definitely abandoned the Weygand plan by 6 P.M. that day and that from that moment on every British unit was moving

19. At the very time Halifax was talking with Bastianini, "the Prime Minister hoped that the Fleet would adopt a vigorously offensive attitude against the Italians if they came into the war" (CAB 69/1).

20. Pownall, *Chief of Staff,* 97.

21. "I am not quite clear what advantages of a decisive character the Germans would gain by starting up a Civil War in Ireland" (PREM 3/129/1). The dinner: Chartwell Household Diary in CA.

west and north, to the coast.) "If we were now to decide on a move to the ports, we must make certain of Dunkirk. There were said to be two French Divisions in Dunkirk, but they were neither of them reliable." (This was not true.)

Then Churchill made a somber and dramatic pronouncement. He "would not be at all surprised if a peace offer was made to the French, having regard to their weak position and to the likelihood of an attack on France by Italy. If France went out of the war, she must, however, make it a condition that our Army was allowed to leave France intact, and to take away its munitions, and that the soil of France was not used for an attack on England. Further, France must retain her Fleet. If an offer were made on these terms, he [the prime minister] would accept it, and he thought that we could hold out in this country once we had got our Army back from France."[22]

This was extraordinary. Churchill knew nothing about the sorry deliberations of the French high council, which had adjourned in Paris only an hour or so before. There is no evidence that Churchill's speculation about a possible peace offering to France was the result of confidential or secret intelligence information that had been made available to him at that moment; it rather seems that this somber speculation was his own. At the same time his phrasing suggests that he had few hopes of extricating the BEF from its situation. That is why one of his last orders to Ironside that day was to tell Brigadier Nicholson in Calais to hold out to the very end: "Defence of Calais to the utmost is of the highest importance to our country and our Army now."[23] That night, he replaced Ironside with General John Dill as chief of the Imperial General Staff. (The official announcement was not made till the twenty-seventh.)

22. CAB 69/1; also in Gilbert, *Companion Volume,* 148–49.
23. CA 4/150.

It was now evident that Sunday, a few hours away, would be an agitated day, to say the least. Churchill requested that the War Cabinet meet as early as 9 A.M.

♦ ♦ ♦

Again it is remarkable how little of all this could be found in the newspapers.[24] There is no evidence that this was due to self-censorship; the private letters and diaries of the newspaper owners show that they were not privy to any information about the prospect of France actually dropping out of the war.

Even so, on 25 May the leading articles and the commentaries in the newspapers were more somber and realistic than they had been during the previous days. For the first time their emphasis was less on the battle in France than on the invasion threat to Britain. The leader in the *Daily Express* read: "The threat to this island grows nearer and nearer. While the people of Britain wait anxiously for news of their soldiers over the Channel, they must prepare for the onslaught which may come upon their own soil." The *Daily Mail*, while praising Churchill (he is "proving himself to us and to the world the supreme leader. He has put heart into his own people and their allies"), "If Hitler consolidates his hold on the Channel ports, the onslaught on these shores will be at hand." One exception was by the military correspondent of the *Daily Herald:* "To evacuate by sea — or force a junction with the French on the Somme. The latter

---

24. About Italy, for instance, the newspapers printed many reports of the Italian preparations for war. The *Daily Express,* 25 May: Count Ciano's speech, telling workers that "they were ready to act with a gun." Another item: in Turin Fascist youths were told, "We shall leave from Turin for the last war of liberation which will break the chains still imposed on this country, which will open the gates of Gibraltar and Suez, and will make the Mediterranean again our sea!"

alternative would seem infinitely preferable and more practicable."
Practicable? By 25 May it was out of the question. The *News Chroni-cle* admitted that Boulogne had fallen: "That is bad news, and the
enemy's latest claims suggest that there may be worse to come."
Even if "the outcome should be that the B.E.F. had to hack its way
through the Nazi ring and leave the Channel ports to the Germans
for the time being [my italics], there would be no need for us to take a
catastrophic view of the position. There can be no large-scale invasion of this country until the Germans have overcome our sea-
power — and they are very far from achieving that." But what about
the air? One photo in the *News Chronicle* showed German prisoners
of war in France. Another, less encouraging one showed a sentry
standing guard beside a road in the south of England; the alarm, to
be rung in an emergency, was a battered oil can.

There was general anxiety about fifth columnists, some of it
funny, like the letters to the editor of the *Times,* printed on 27 May
by a J. M. Darroch: "Sir — It was with much pleasure and amuse-
ment that I observed this morning that you have seen fit to publish
the news of Sir Oswald Mosley's arrest in the fifth column of today's
issue." A reporter from the *Daily Telegraph* wormed his way into a
meeting of "the Link," the Anglo-German society: "Still Unbroken."
There were about forty people. "The lecturer asserted that the war
was caused by international financiers. . . . The Germans were only
'technically' our enemies." In the *Daily Mirror:* "Shipping circles in
Bristol are concerned that two Germans, mother and son, are still
allowed to carry on their business as foreigners at Avonmouth."
(The mother and the son were Jewish refugees.) Mixed in with this
anxiety about spies and foreigners and refugees was a certain per-
sistent provinciality. In the *Daily Mirror:* "Instead of playing tennis
or going on the river ten Balliol undergraduates went in a van lent by
Lord Nuffield to a farm nearby, . . . where they began a spell of

hoeing." And in a letter to the editor, two girls in the "Land Army" entreated: "Our grouse is that we are ashamed to wear our uniforms on leave in London because no one knows who or what we are. People say we look like out-of-work cowboys. Won't you put in a good word for us?"

Yet in the list "Army Dead" in the *Times* some women were listed.

The picture of British morale that emerges from the day's newspapers is different from that of the opinion reports, which are grimmer in tone. There exists an extensive confidential paper prepared by the Ministry of Information on 25 May: *Public Opinion: The Present Crisis.*[25] Under the heading "Morale": "There is definite evidence of increasing confusion. Today the strongest optimists (working-class men) are often qualifying their remarks with slight suspicion or doubt about the way things are developing." They are of course critical of the French: "Depression is quite definitely up, but on the whole the main trend is toward fatalism, as if people's minds were prepared for almost anything in the way of bad news. Complacency [has] practically disappeared. . . . There are further reports which show that the morale of women is considerably lower than that of the men. The King's speech had a steadying but not a deep effect." (King George VI had broadcast to the nation the previous night; many people commented favorably on his delivery, since the king was known for his habit of stuttering.) "Many people expressed the opinion that the mobilisation of man-power and woman-power is still not being tackled realistically." Under the heading "Class and Sex Differences in Morale": "Upper classes show more disquiet and slightly less optimism than working class. There is more *doubt* among the working class. . . . Tension is greatest among middle and

25. INF 1/264, No. 8 Secret.

upper class women, and least among working class men. . . . A number of social workers consulted are of the opinion that working class women are more likely to show panic than other classes of the community."

There follows a sheet summing up "Rumours," and then "Points from Regions": "Although there seems to be general confidence about the ultimate outcome of the war, there is considerable confusion in most of the Regions about the present military situation in France. Coincident with this is a feeling of tension and expectation of a coming counter attack; unless this materialises fairly soon the effect on morale would seem to be to increase general uneasiness. At the moment, however, the public on the whole seems to be fairly calm and determined." Bristol: "The effect of Haw Haw [the Britisher broadcasting pro-German propaganda from Germany] is considered to be extremely insidious, and this danger is underestimated by the BBC and the Government, who do not fully appreciate to what extent this propaganda is believed." Birmingham: the king's speech ("a grand effort") was greatly appreciated, but "in some sections of the community there is a rather defeatist feeling among people who are not very well off and who have not much idea of what we shall lose if we do not win the war." Manchester: the king's speech was "just what was wanted." Reading: "Although tension is increased here there is no suggestion of panic, but the continued absence of the eagerly awaited Allied offensive is causing a good deal of apprehension. There is a growing anxiety about bombing and parachute troops — fears continue to be fed by rumour."

"The action taken against potential Fifth Columnists is strongly approved. . . . These precautions should be carried to even greater lengths." Cardiff: "Feeling is definitely disturbed by our apparent inability to check the German advance, and by the possibility that this may mean that our own troops will be cut off, but never-the-less there is confidence in our ultimate success."

On 25 May, Mass-Observation, somewhat unusually, set out a report on people's morale in statistical terms:

	Males (%)	Females (%)
Disquiet	27	31
Optimism	30	18
Doubt (Don't Know)	21	30

Disquiet was higher among the upper middle class (40 to 25 percent) than among the lower class and artisan samples of the population; optimism was about even (23 to 25 percent) between the two groups; the number responding "don't know" was higher among the lower and artisan classes and higher among their females. The daily Mass-Observation survey, which was also transmitted to the Ministry of Information, largely accorded with the ministry's morale survey: "People are becoming distinctly confused today, and the strongest optimists, the working-class males, are today often qualifying their remarks with some slight suspicion or doubt as to the way things are developing." Some people cannot understand how the Germans can advance as they are doing without being cut off. Plenty believe that all this development is part of our strategy."

"Depression is quite definitely up," the survey concluded, "but on the whole the main trend is for people to be rather fatalistic, as if their minds were prepared for almost anything now in the way of *bad news*. A large number of people today are finding themselves unable to express any opinion or to know what to think. . . . On the whole, the quality of optimism has violently declined, and the quality of pessimism deepened. The public mind is in a chaotic condition and ready to be plunged into the depths of an utterly bewildered, shocked, almost unbelieving dismay. The whole structure of national belief would seem to be rocking gently."[26]

Compared with many other reports, some of them cited above, this last summary statement, suggesting as it does a radical change in mood, seems to have been exaggerated. For once, the words of Virginia Woolf in her diary, where this withdrawn and often solipsistic woman otherwise gave very little space to the great political and military events of that time, sum up the situation and the feeling of the day: "The [Germans] seem youthful, fresh, inventive. We plod behind."[27]

26. FR 138.

27. *The Diary of Virginia Woolf,* 287, 288: "Today's rumour is the Nun in the bus who pays her fare with a man's hand."

CHAPTER FOUR

Sunday, 26 May

An agitated day. – Three meetings of the War Cabinet. – Chamberlain,
Halifax, Churchill. – Disagreements between Halifax and Churchill. –
Scarcity of news: "A mandate to delay judgment and not to worry." –
"In Westminster Abbey."

A gloomy day, in more than one way: for the first time in many a
day it rained.

In early April there had been some talk of a National Day of
Prayer. The archbishop of Canterbury had thought it inadvisable because it could be misinterpreted. Now, along with all the churches,
he endorsed it. The king had spoken of it in his broadcast of 23 May.[1]
So had the newspapers. "Let Us Pray" was an article on the front
page of the *Daily Express* on Saturday: "It must mean something

---

1. On 19 May an extraordinary ceremony took place in Paris. The digni-
taries of the agnostic Third Republic gathered in the cool vault of Notre
Dame.

tomorrow." At ten o'clock on Sunday morning the king, the queen, and the highest personages of the empire arrived in Westminster Abbey. The king and queen carried gas masks. Wilhelmina, queen of the Netherlands, came with them. Someone shouted: "Long live the Netherlands!" Wilhelmina dropped a curtsey. There was a long queue outside. Churchill made it clear to his household that he and Mrs. Churchill would be able to attend for no longer than ten to thirty minutes. Indeed they left early, in the middle of the service, for there was plenty for him to do.

The events of this grave Sunday were so many and complicated that, before their reconstruction and analysis, their sequence ought to be sorted out and summed up briefly. We have seen that Churchill requested a meeting of the War Cabinet at the unusual hour of 9 A.M. on this Sunday. One hour later came the high service in Westminster Abbey. Meanwhile, Reynaud and a French delegation arrived in London. At noon Halifax saw the Italian ambassador again. Then he lunched with Chamberlain. Churchill had a long lunch with Reynaud in Admiralty House. He returned to 10 Downing Street for another cabinet at 2 P.M. After about forty minutes Churchill asked Halifax to go over to Admiralty House to meet with Reynaud. Churchill, Chamberlain, and Greenwood followed him twenty or so minutes later. A few minutes after four o'clock Reynaud left for France. The War Cabinet members stayed. There was another cabinet meeting in Admiralty House at five o'clock, ending at half past six. At eight Churchill dined with Ismay and Eden.

The War Cabinet session at 9 A.M. began with Churchill's account of the situation with the French and with the Belgians. He had a letter from his personal representative in Paris, General Edward Spears — all bad news about France and the French. The king of Belgium was making ready to capitulate. Churchill's envoy to the king, Sir Roger Keyes, had sent a telegram whose essence was that "King

Leopold had written to King George VI to explain his motive in remaining with his army and people if the Belgian Army became encircled and the capitulation of the Belgian Army became inevitable."

The gist of all this was summed up by Churchill: "It seems from all the evidence available that we might have to face a situation in which the French were going to collapse, and that we must do our best to extricate the British Expeditionary Force from northern France."

Then Churchill played an important card. A few days before he had asked the chiefs of staff "to consider the situation which would arise if the French would drop out of the war."

> In the event of France being unable to continue in the war and becoming neutral, with the Germans holding their present position and the Belgian army being forced to capitulate after assisting the British Expeditionary Force to reach the coast; in the event of terms offered to Britain which would place her entirely at the mercy of Germany through disarmament, cession of naval bases in the Orkneys etc.; what are the prospects of our continuing the war alone against Germany and probably Italy. Can the Navy and the Air Force hold out reasonable hopes of preventing serious invasion, and could the forces gathered in this Island cope with raids from the air involving detachments not greater than 10,000 men; it being observed that a prolongation of British resistance might be very dangerous for Germany engaged in holding down the greater part of Europe.

The answer of the chiefs of staff has since become a historic document of first importance, well known to students of the period. Entitled "British Strategy in a Certain Eventuality," it was a long paper.[2] It presumed the worst possible conditions — and, by 25 May, an increasingly plausible situation: the French making peace with Germany, Italy entering the war, Europe and French North Africa under German control, and the loss of most of the British Expeditionary Force still struggling in northern France and Belgium. Still — even in these conditions Britain could hold out, *if* the United States would support Britain increasingly, eventually entering the war, and *if* the Royal Air Force, together with the navy, would remain in control over Britain and thus "prevent Germany from carrying out a serious sea-borne invasion of this country." In this they were to be proved right. The rest of the document dealt with the question of whether Germany could be ultimately defeated. On 25 May this could not be even remotely envisaged. The chiefs of staff assumed that Germany's economic situation was to be plagued by shortages of raw materials. Together with air attacks and revolts in the occupied countries, Germany could be defeated — at some time in the future, and with American help. In this assessment the chiefs of staff were wrong rather than right. They — much like Attlee and Greenwood in the War Cabinet, and to a considerable extent Chamberlain, too — not only overestimated but were altogether mistaken about the economic "factors" handicapping Germany.[3] But that

2. CAB 66-7 [W.P. (40) 168; also C.O.S. (40) 390]. Bell, *A Certain Eventuality*, 31: "a euphemistic wording regularly used in such papers in place of a direct reference to a French collapse."

3. This assumption — very much mistaken — was predominant in the Board of Economic Warfare. "Its main activities are recorded in a number of reasonably honest, though regrettably bland, official publications, such as W. N. Medlicott's *The Economic Blockade* (London, 1952), whose first sentence reads: 'Too much, it is now agreed, was expected of the blockade in

is not our concern here. The crux was "the immediate problem [of] . . . how to get through the next few months, with the Germans across the Channel and no effective allies. On this the Chiefs of Staff offered a reasoned case for hope."[4]

We must, however, consider that on this Sunday, one so closely packed with dramatic events, the War Cabinet members did not have the time to peruse this long document in detail. And before copies of this secret paper were circulated, there occurred the first open clash of opinion between Halifax and Churchill.

Halifax said that "in the dark picture which had been presented there was one brighter spot in that the dispute on the rights and wrongs of Lord Gort's action in drawing back had now been satisfactorily cleared up and there would be no recriminations on that point." Then he came to "the broader issue. We had to face the fact that it was not so much now a question of imposing a complete defeat upon Germany but of safeguarding the independence of our own Empire and if possible that of France."

"In this connection," he told the cabinet about his interview with the Italian ambassador the night before, "Signor Bastianini had clearly made soundings as to the prospect of our agreeing to a conference. The Ambassador had said that Signor Mussolini's principal

---

the Second World War? Indeed, Great Expectations reigned, at least on paper, in the Bleak House of the London School of Economics where the new ministry had its home at first. . . . [But then] Chamberlain's war strategy, too, rested on his trust in the efficacy of the blockade; he 'did not believe that the enemy could face a second winter.' . . . [Yet] until the middle of 1944 the German economy had no general difficulties in providing its war materials" (Lukacs, *The Last European War*, 232–33).

4. Bell, *A Certain Eventuality*, 50.

wish was to secure peace in Europe." He (Halifax) "had replied that peace and security in Europe were equally our main object, and we should naturally be prepared to consider any proposals which might lead to this, provided our liberty and independence were assured. The French had been informed of this approach by the Italian Ambassador. Signor Bastianini had asked for a further interview this morning, and he might have fresh proposals to put forward."

Churchill said that peace and security would not be achieved under a German domination of Europe: "That we could never accept. We must ensure our complete liberty and independence. He was opposed to any negotiations which might lead to a derogation of our rights and power."

Chamberlain now said that he "thought it very probable that Italy might send an ultimatum to France very shortly, saying that unless she would agree to a conference, Italy would come in on Germany's side. This would bring very heavy pressure to bear on the French." There followed some confusing talk about Italy. Attlee "thought that Mussolini would be very nervous of Germany emerging as the predominant power in Europe." (This was not so.) Attlee added that he had not yet read the papers of the chiefs of staff "as to our prospects of holding out if the French collapsed." Halifax made a somewhat obscure statement. He pointed out that if the French intended to come to terms, "they had a very strong card to play if they made it clear to Hitler that they were bound not to make a separate peace." (Why?) "They might use this as a powerful lever to obtain favourable terms which might be of great value to us, if it was Hitler's object to break the alliance."

At that moment copies of another paper by the chiefs of staff were handed to the members of the cabinet about the prospects of Britain going on with the war single-handed. "It had been drawn up simply for the purpose of providing arguments to deter the French from capitulating and to strengthen their will to continue to fight."[5] Chamberlain thought that Italy was important. "Was it possible to ask the French whether Italy could be bought off? This might at least keep matters going." Churchill "agreed that this point was worth bearing in mind." Halifax then said that, from reading the chiefs of staffs' paper, he gathered that the entire issue "of our ability to carry on the war single-handed against Germany would depend on the main on our being able to establish and maintain air superiority over the Germans."

The chief of the air staff, who was present throughout the meeting, said that the issue was "not our obtaining air superiority over the Germans, but on our preventing the Germans from achieving such air superiority as would enable them to invade this country." There was some discussion of this, with Halifax suggesting that once France collapsed the Germans would "no longer need large land forces. They would be free to switch the bulk of their effort to air production." He also "suggested that in the last resort we should ask the French to put their factories out of gear." Chamberlain must have felt that this was nugatory: "Whatever undertakings of this character we might extract from the French would be worthless, since the terms of peace which the Germans would propose would inevitably prevent their fulfilment." Churchill "agreed. It was to be expected, however, that the Germans would make the terms of any peace offer as attractive as possible to the French, but lay emphasis on the fact that their quarrel was not with France but with England."[6]

Then he asked the War Cabinet to convene again at 2 P.M., after

5. C.O.S. 40(391), not identical with 390.
6. CAB 65/13 WM 139.

his lunch with Reynaud. They adjourned, Churchill and Chamberlain hurrying to Westminster Abbey. Halifax went back to the Foreign Office, where Bastianini came to see him. Cadogan, who was present, wrote in his diary: "Nothing to be got out of [Bastianini]. He's an ass — and a timid one at that."[7] Then Halifax had a quick lunch with Chamberlain.

Churchill had a long lunch with Reynaud at Admiralty House. Reynaud was constrained to present Churchill with a general view of the near hopelessness of the French military situation, largely in accord with what Weygand and Pétain had insisted upon in their high council the night before. Churchill said that Britain would go on alone. "We would rather go down fighting than be enslaved to Germany." Yet underlying their discussion, which was not unfriendly — Reynaud, who was an Anglophile, respected and admired Churchill — was an understanding that their governments were divided. This, of course, was less so with the British than with the French. Reynaud "had hinted that he himself would not sign peace terms imposed upon France, but that he might be forced to resign, or might feel he ought to resign" — which eventually came about, three weeks to the day. Churchill knew about Weygand and Pétain, though he was not yet fully aware of the defeatism of the former. Nor was he quite aware of what another member of the French delegation had sensed, or had pretended to sense. Colonel Villelume was

7. Cadogan, *Diaries,* 290. (Late on Saturday night Gladwyn Jebb had met with Paresci.) Bastianini was "timid" because he feared Mussolini, who had already instructed his ambassadors in London and Paris and Washington not to engage in substantial negotiations. There is no record of his short conversations with Halifax on Sunday, unless it is subsumed within the report he drafted about their talk on the previous day — which may have been the reason of the relative lateness of his summary dispatch to Rome. See above, p. 93.

Reynaud's principal military aide. That evening he wrote in his diary, "Halifax . . . shows his understanding; Churchill, prisoner of his habit of blustering, was absolutely negative."[8]

At 2 P.M. the War Cabinet convened again. Churchill gave a lengthy and rather precise account of what Reynaud had said and what he had told Reynaud. He then suggested that Halifax go over and see Reynaud, who was still at Admiralty House; Churchill, Chamberlain, and Attlee would follow a few minutes later. Halifax would talk with Reynaud about the chances of buying off Mussolini. Did Churchill wish to avoid Halifax, since the latter might state his case before the others in the War Cabinet? We cannot tell. And Halifax did not leave yet. "A short further discussion ensued whether we should make any approach to Italy." Halifax "favoured this course, and thought that the last thing that Signor Mussolini wanted was to see Herr Hitler dominating Europe. He would be anxious, if he could, to persuade Herr Hitler to take a more reasonable attitude." Churchill "doubted whether anything would come of an approach to Italy, but said that the matter was one which the War Cabinet would have to consider."

The open disagreement between Halifax and Churchill had now

8. Villelume, *Journal d'une défaite,* 356. Alexis Léger, the secretary-general of the Foreign Ministry, inclined to Churchill. This did not matter much, though somehow it was made known to the arch-appeaser Horace Wilson, whom Churchill had thrown out of Downing Street a fortnight before and who had then written that "Léger was violently anti-German, equally violently anti-Italian, and he must bear much of the responsibility for the failure to take advantage of the opportunities offered from time to time, by either Hitler or Mussolini for some kind of rapprochement." That would come to Churchill's attention in October 1941, when he was threatened by another potential collapse, that of the Russian army. Horace Wilson Papers, CAB 127/158.

become evident. Halifax no longer wished merely to state his views; now he wanted to extract a commitment from Churchill: "We had to face the fact that it was not so much now a question of imposing a complete defeat upon Germany but of safeguarding the independence of our Empire. . . . We should naturally be prepared to consider any proposals which might lead to this, provided our liberty and independence were assured. . . . If he [Churchill] was satisfied that matters vital to the independence of this country were unaffected," would he be "prepared to discuss such terms?"

At this juncture Churchill knew that he could not answer with a categorical no. He said that he "would be thankful to get out of our present difficulties on such terms, provided we retained the essentials and the elements of our vital strength, *even at the cost of some territory*" — an extraordinary admission (my italics).[9] He then added that he did not believe in the prospect of such a deal. Chamberlain did not say much. Then with Churchill and Greenwood he departed to Admiralty House to join Halifax and Reynaud, who were discussing the approach to Mussolini. Reynaud left after four o'clock.

Churchill now asked the War Cabinet to stay on in Admiralty House. The record of this day's third, fairly dramatic meeting of the War Cabinet is preceded by two significantly cryptic notes: "After M. Reynaud's departure, an informal Meeting of War Cabinet Ministers was held in Admiralty House." (Why "informal"?) Also, perhaps more significantly: "This record does not cover the first quarter of an hour of the discussion, during which the Secretary [Sir Edward Bridges] was not present."[10] Such conditions of secrecy had no precedent in the modern history of Britain. Then the Secretary came in and Churchill began.

9. See below, pp. 116–17, 120.
10. CAB 65/13, WM 140.

"We were in a different position from France. In the first place, we still had powers of resistance and attack [?] which they had not. In the second place, they would be likely to be offered decent terms by Germany, which we would not. If France could not defend herself, it was better that she should get out of the war rather than that she should drag us into a settlement which involved intolerable terms. There was no limit to the terms which Germany would impose upon us if she had her way. From one point of view, he would rather France was out of the war before she was broken up, and retained the position of a strong neutral whose factories could not be used against us."

Attlee said that Hitler "was working to a time-limit, and he had to win by the end of the year." Chamberlain agreed. (Both were wrong — again, due to their overestimation of the economic factors.)

Churchill said that "he hoped that France would hang on. At the same time we must take care not to be forced into a weak position in which we went to Signor Mussolini and invited him, to go to Herr Hitler and ask him to treat us nicely. We must not get entangled in a position of that kind before we had been involved in serious fighting."

Now Halifax spoke. He "did not disagree with this view," but "he attached perhaps rather more importance than the Prime Minister to the desirability of allowing France to try out the possibilities of European equilibrium.[11] He was not quite convinced that the Prime Minister's diagnosis was correct and that it was Herr Hitler's interest to insist on outrageous terms. On this lay-out it might be possi-

11. "Equilibrium"? See below about Halifax and the Peace of Amiens, pp. 125–26.

ble to save France from the wreck." Churchill disagreed. Halifax "said that he was not so sure." He "thought that we might say to Signor Mussolini that if there was any suggestion of terms which affected our independence, we should not look at them for a moment. If, however, Signor Mussolini was alarmed as we felt he must be in regard to Herr Hitler's power, and was prepared to look at matters from the point of view of the balance of power, then we might consider Italian claims. At any rate, he could see no harm in trying this line of approach."

Chamberlain now sat on the fence. He "thought that Mussolini could only take an independent line if Herr Hitler were disposed to conform to the line which Signor Mussolini indicated. The problem was a very difficult one, and it was right to talk it out from every point of view." Chamberlain did not think that Reynaud had a case for buying Mussolini off: "For one thing, the only advantage we should get was that France would be able to move away ten divisions now on the Italian front. Signor Mussolini would get something for nothing, and what was offered would be only the starting-point for new demands." This was correct. Yet: "Another method of approach would be if the French told Signor Mussolini that he must consider the future of Europe, including his own future. Italy was in no safer position than any other country. If Signor Mussolini was prepared to collaborate with us in getting tolerable terms, then we would be prepared to discuss Italian demands with him." Hadn't Churchill said "that it was undesirable that France should be in a position to say that we had stood between her and a tolerable settlement?" Still, Chamberlain agreed with Churchill that we might be better off without France, "provided we could obtain safeguards on particular points. This was certainly a point of view which deserved serious consideration."

Churchill "thought that it was best to decide nothing until we saw how much of the Army we could re-embark from France. The operation might be a great failure. On the other hand, our troops might well fight magnificently, and we might save a considerable portion of the Force. A good deal of the re-embarkation would be carried out by day. This would afford a real test of air superiority, since the Germans would attempt to bomb the ships and boats." (Attlee "thought that the Germans might well attempt some diversion against this country while we were engaged in re-embarking the Force.") This was the first indication that what was to happen at Dunkirk was predominant in Churchill's mind.

This was not so with Halifax. He came back to the Italian matter. He read out the account of his talk with Bastianini. Churchill answered that "his general comment on the suggested approach to Signor Mussolini was that it implied that if we were prepared to give Germany back her colonies and to make certain concessions in the Mediterranean, it was possible for us to get out of our present difficulties. He thought that no such option was open to us. For example, the terms offered would certainly prevent us from completing our re-armament." Halifax did not quite agree. Churchill said that "Herr Hitler thought that he had the whip hand. The only thing to do was to show him that he could not conquer this country. If, on M. Reynaud's showing, France could not continue, we must part company. At the same time, he did not raise objection to some approach being made to Signor Mussolini."

What this meant was that Churchill, at least momentarily, thought that he had to make *some* kind of concession to Halifax. There followed a discussion of what might be offered to Mussolini. Greenwood "thought that Signor Mussolini would be out to get Malta, Gibraltar and Suez. He felt sure that the negotiations would break down; but Herr Hitler would get to know of them, and it might have a bad effect on our prestige." Chamberlain generally agreed. Halifax "thought that this was a good argument against mentioning particular matters in the approach." Chamberlain "thought that Signor Mussolini would say that he knew what he wanted, but was only prepared to deal as part of a general settlement." This was so; but now Halifax came to the essence of his argument. He "thought that if we got to the point of discussing the terms of a general settlement and found that we could obtain terms which did not postulate the destruction of our independence, we would be *foolish* if we did not accept them."[12] And now Churchill felt that he could not oppose Halifax unconditionally. The War Cabinet agreed to ask Halifax to prepare a draft of his "Suggested Approach to Italy." At the same time Churchill gained a point: the cabinet agreed that the next day Archibald Sinclair, the secretary of state for air, "as head of the Liberal Party, would be invited to be present when this matter was discussed." Sinclair was a supporter of Churchill.

The rest of the meeting involved discussions about Belgium and Ireland. Chamberlain asked what information should be given out to the Dominions. Churchill said that nothing should be divulged as yet, except that the French had agreed to the move of the BEF to the coast.[13]

The meeting lasted for about an hour and a half. It was a "very

---

12. The italics are mine. See also Esnouf, "British Government War Aims and Attitudes": "These were strong words for the normally mildly mannered and spoken Halifax, and they show both the depth of his feeling and the danger of the policy which he could see Churchill was determined to pursue" (225).

13. CAB 65/13 [WM 139].

jumpy" meeting (Halifax wrote in his diary), especially near the end, with secretaries coming in and out, bringing dispatches about Belgium, Ireland, and so on. Toward the end of the meeting, Halifax produced his "Suggested Approach to Signor Mussolini," prepared after his meeting with Reynaud.[14] Its essence was: "If Signor Mussolini will co-operate with us in securing a settlement of all European questions which safeguard[s] the independence and the security of the Allies, and could be the basis of a just and durable peace for Europe, we will undertake at once to discuss, with the desire to find solutions, the matters in which Signor Mussolini is primarily interested." (Somewhat disingenuously, Halifax suggested that this kind of phrasing was Reynaud's, whereas it was really Halifax's.) This was now coupled with the text of a joint British-French appeal in Washington to President Roosevelt, asking that he inform Mussolini of the French and British willingness to consider certain Italian claims, "to be dependent of course on Italy not entering the war against the Allies."[15] The memorandum had a postscript reporting the opinion of the British ambassador to Rome, Sir Percy Loraine, to the effect that neither this approach nor any attempt by Roosevelt would do any good. Yet "the situation could hardly be made worse by the approach suggested by M. Reynaud, and that the first consideration there set out must be very present to Signor Mussolini's mind." (That "first consideration" in the memorandum was "a frank explanation of the position in which Signor Mussolini will be placed if the Germans establish domination in Europe.") Yet there was a

14. CAB 66/7 [W.P. (40) 170].

15. Three days earlier Halifax saw Joseph Kennedy, who was utterly pessimistic about England's chances and, as usual, contemptuous of Churchill. Kennedy wrote Roosevelt in the same vein.

difference in the emphasis of the approaches. Reynaud's main purpose was to try buying Mussolini off; Halifax's, to try inducing Mussolini to mediate with Hitler.[16]

◆ ◆ ◆

Let us now leave Halifax and Churchill for a moment and consider Chamberlain. Cadogan was summoned to Admiralty House for the 5 P.M. meeting. In his diary he wrote: Churchill "seemed to think we might almost be better off if France *did* pull out and we could concentrate on defence here. Not sure he's right. He [is] against final appeal, which Reynaud wanted, to Muss. He may be right there. Settled nothing much. W.S.C. too rambling and romantic and sentimental and temperamental. Old Neville still best of the lot."[17] Best of the lot or not, Chamberlain, in his handwritten diary, tells us much about the atmosphere and about some of the details of that crucial day: "*May 26*. Blackest day of all. . . . This was the National Day of Prayer. I could hardly attend to the service with this load on my mind." About the 5 P.M. cabinet: "Halifax said why not suggest that [Mussolini's] own independence would be threatened if France and G.B. [!] collapsed but if he would use his influence to discuss terms which did not menace our independence and offered a

16. G. N. Esnouf: "Indeed these two matters, of an approach to buy off Italy and one to induce Mussolini to mediate with Hitler, were closely linked despite their separate motives and ramifications. Because of this, the Cabinet discussions of both matters were often intertwined, so that it is not always clear from the minutes which proposal is being referred to. Yet to distinguish between them is crucial. Buying off Italy facilitated the war against Germany, Italian mediation meant its end, such was the enormity of the discussions of 26 to 28 May" ("British Government War Aims and Attitudes," 223).

17. Cadogan, *Diaries,* 290.

prospect of a just and durable settlement of Europe we would try to meet his own claims. . . . The P.M. disliked any move toward Musso.[18] It was incredible that Hitler would consent to any terms that we could accept—though if we could get out of this jam by giving up Malta & Gibraltar & some African colonies he would jump at it. But the only safe way was to convince Hitler that he couldn't beat us. . . . I supported this view, Attlee said hardly anything but seemed to be with Winston. . . . We hear Hitler had told Mussolini that he does not want him in as he can manage France by himself.[19] If so, he evidently cannot be bought off. . . . But it is a terrible position for France and ourselves. The most horrible in our history."[20]

At this moment in his long life Neville Chamberlain was already a very sick man. He may not have known that; the diagnosis of his cancer occurred a month later. But—notwithstanding all the justifiable gloom and doom of his diary, which he wrote with a strong and untrembling nervous hand at the end of that very long, very tiring day—he was not weak. His situation in the War Cabinet was central. He sat—literally as well as figuratively—between Halifax and Churchill. Had he sided with Halifax, Churchill's position would have been not only very difficult but perhaps untenable. But it was

18. Esnouf cites an unsigned note by Churchill of 26 or 27 May, in Churchill's handwriting, in PREM 3/174/4, 11–3: the Italian move would lead "to an armistice and conference under the conditions of our being at Hitler's mercy. . . . Such a conference would only end in weakening fatally our power to resist the terrible terms which will almost certainly be imposed, if not upon France, at any rate upon Britain."

19. How did they know this? In 1940 and for some years before, both the Italian and the British secret services were able to decrypt and read many of each other's documents. Yet such a suggestion from Hitler to Mussolini could hardly be extracted from Hitler's letter of 25 May (see above, p. 95).

20. Chamberlain Diary, NC A 24/2.

not only because of Chamberlain's literally crucial position that we must eschew the imputation of weakness. When I wrote above that on one occasion he "sat on the fence," balancing between Halifax and Churchill, his statements show a considerable strength of his views. There were two elements in these. One was his, perhaps belated, but essentially substantial, realization of what Hitler was: of what could, and of what could not, be expected from him. In this respect Chamberlain had become more realistic and less willing to compromise than Halifax. There was now a nearly complete reversal of their respective views of Hitler nineteen months (before Munich) or even eight months before, when it was he, Chamberlain, who had been inclined to give Hitler some benefit of doubt and Halifax much less so, if any at all; Chamberlain had learned much since that time. But there was another element, too—perhaps an even more important one. This was Chamberlain's new relationship with Churchill. Yes, Churchill was dependent on him, even after becoming prime minister, because of Chamberlain's support by the majority of the Conservative Party. Yes, Churchill had asked him to be in charge of important matters of government. (When, on 16 May, Churchill had had to fly to Paris, he said, "Neville, please mind the shop!") But there was even more to it than that. After the May crisis, Churchill wrote to Lloyd George (who hated Chamberlain): "I have received a very great deal of help from Chamberlain. His kindness and courtesy to me in our new relations have touched me. I have joined hands with him and must act with perfect loyalty."[21] Note the phrase "new relations." This change was indeed new—and more than an improvement. Its main architect (if that is the word) was Churchill, inspired less by calculation than by magnanimity. Their enmities and suspicions had begun to dissolve

21. Quoted in Dilks, "The Twilight War."

from the very moment when Churchill had become a member of Chamberlain's government—from the very first day of the war. Soon Chamberlain would confide to his wife and sister that Churchill's loyalty was unexceptionable. And after 10 May it was not only that Chamberlain knew he was now subordinate to the new prime minister. There was, too, Churchill's instant and generous offer to the Chamberlains to continue living at 10 Downing Street. Churchill's magnanimity was something to which, perhaps because of his temperament and background, Chamberlain had been unaccustomed. Indeed to some extent it may have surprised him. He not only welcomed but appreciated it and responded to it, which is to his credit; and this was more than a weary gratitude for courtesies that had been offered to an old man.

◆ ◆ ◆

It was thus that, during what was probably the greatest crisis for Britain in long centuries, Churchill did not have to face opposition from Chamberlain. Few people outside the War Cabinet were aware of that.[22] This does not mean that Churchill and Chamberlain now saw everything in the same way. They were, after all, different in their temperaments and also in their vision. Next to Britain, Churchill mainly envisaged Europe; Chamberlain, perhaps, the Empire. Churchill was convinced that a British acceptance of the German dominion of Europe was intolerable, and not only because of the security of Great Britain. Chamberlain knew less about Europe than Churchill did and, save for Europe's effects on Britain's security, was less inspired by what happened there. What they had come to agree on was that Hitler could not be trusted; indeed, that he must be rejected; and in these crucial days, that was enough.

22. See Dalton, above, p. 5. Many supporters of Churchill suspected that Chamberlain, rather than Halifax, was irresolute.

This was not the case with Halifax. But before returning to an analysis of Halifax's views, perhaps we should permit ourselves one more word about his character, especially in view of his relationship with the king, which did contain a possible political consideration. King George VI liked Halifax and offered him many private and personal favors. "Diffident, moral, family men, the King and Halifax both had speech impediments, which caused them to dislike microphones and distrust Churchill's ebullient grandiloquence. They had many good qualities in common, and their view on appeasement and politics in general largely coincided, but they were the wrong type of men to lead Britain in a world war. Fortunately, Halifax appreciated this fact about himself" (Andrew Roberts). "Halifax had a reputation for sound judgment, and never did he exercise it better than when he refused the Premiership on 9 May 1940. Halifax's new role was to work with Chamberlain in the War Cabinet to restrain Churchill, and it must have been a relief for him to know that, if the new Prime Minister did turn out to justify their worst fears, the ultimate prerogative to dismiss him lay with a monarch whom the 'Respectable Tendency' could trust to act in their best interests."[23] And Churchill knew that.

The question that we must raise at this moment is this: Now, a fortnight after Churchill's assumption of the premiership, was Halifax's judgment sound? He had come to believe that, for the sake of England's survival, the attempt to inquire about peace terms should not be avoided, and that here Churchill, carried away perhaps by his flamboyance and other qualities alien to Halifax, was wrong; indeed, that perhaps Churchill ought to be stopped in his tracks. But the purpose behind this was not political ambition: there is not the slightest indication that, were Churchill thwarted or eventually

23. Roberts, *Eminent Churchillians,* 37.

removed, Halifax wished to take his place. He was motivated by patriotism, not ambition. Halifax was not a defeatist, nor was he an intriguer. He *was* a seasoned watcher of the tides of events and of the tides of British opinion. He was a very British type, in the sense that he know how to adjust his mind to circumstances rather than to attempt to adjust the circumstances to his ideas. This does not mean that he was a hypocrite or an opportunist — except in the habitual Anglo-Saxon way, which is not really Machiavellian since the innate practice of that kind of English hypocrisy often serves purposes that are higher than individual prestige or profit.[24]

And now: was Halifax a typical British conservative? By this I mean not his situation within the Conservative Party but whether he could be considered a "conservative," with a lowercase *c:* was he an exemplar of British conservatism? Yes and no. Yes: because of his background and habits and his personal and social inclinations. No: because his views about Britain's position in the world were more Whiggish than Tory, more pragmatically rather than historically minded, and certainly not Burkean. An important clue to this may be found in one of his, generally unremarked, speeches. The title of his address, "British Foreign Policy: Past, Present, and Future," is telling, and so is the date, 24 February 1939, that is, well *after* his conversion from appeasement to resistance to the Third Reich.[25] In the central argument of his speech Halifax refuted Burke. Burke had said in 1792, about the French Revolution, "It is with an armed doctrine that we are at war." Halifax said, "But that, however, is precisely what we were not." Note that "precisely." He cited Pitt, and

24. "Which is, too, why the Anglophobe phrase 'perfidious Albion' is incorrect" (Lukacs, *The Duel*, 89).

25. The text is not in the Halifax Papers in York but in the Churchill Archives, Cambridge.

he cited Castlereagh in 1820: "When the territorial balance in Europe is disturbed [England] can interfere with effect, but she is the last government in Europe which can be expected or can venture to commit itself on any question of abstract character."[26] Leaving aside the consideration that Edmund Burke, ideologically opposed as he was to the French Revolution, was very far from being an abstractionist, Halifax's statement of the principles of British foreign policy make it clear that he was thinking in the usual terms of the balance of power.[27] And, in a way, it was still in terms of a balance of power that Halifax saw the war in May 1940. It is interesting that it was Halifax who suggested on 16 May that Churchill write a personal letter to Mussolini.[28] At the same time he — unlike Chamberlain — was very willing to improve relations with Stalin's Russia. On that same day of 16 May he consulted Sir Stafford Cripps about Russia (and China). "I like Cripps very much."

Whether Halifax knew the history of the Napoleonic era as well as did Churchill we cannot tell. Yet the position advocated by Halifax in May 1940 resembled that of the Foxite and Hollandite Whigs in 1802, who were in favor of the armistice with Bonaparte, the 1802 Peace of Amiens. (There was, however, a difference: the Foxite and Hollandite Whigs in 1802 had a definite respect, even a touch of admiration, for Bonaparte, whereas Halifax had no such ideological sentiments for Hitler.) What Halifax did not understand was that,

26. It may be argued that this statement was even more Canningite than Castlereaghian.

27. In this respect it is curious to note that it was Churchill who, because of his concern with the European balance of power, was vocal about the threat of German armament and potential aggression as early as 1933, whereas Halifax and the appeasers, even much later, were not.

28. On 6 April 1940: "I still adhere to my view that [Mussolini] is going to bark more than bite" (Halifax Papers, A.7.8.3). Halifax was wrong.

unlike Bonaparte in 1802, Hitler would have been contemptuous of the kind of Britain that would inquire for terms. And that Churchill understood very well.

And in 1802 Britain still had, if not actual, then potential Allied Powers in Europe. Unlike in 1802, in 1940 Britain, after France, would have none. Unlike Churchill, Halifax never thought much of the French or of the French army; as early as December 1939 he said in the cabinet that if ever the French dropped out, "we should not be able to carry on the war by ourselves." The night before 26 May he wrote in his diary about how awful the collapse of the French army was, "the one firm rock on which everybody has been willing to build for the last two years." (For "everybody," read Churchill.) In this respect the British historian Sheila Lawlor, in *Churchill and the Politics of War, 1940–1941,* is wrong. She writes of the "superficial differences (which were really the best way to deal with the French)" between Halifax and Churchill in May 1940, concluding that "Halifax rejected the peace moves and negotiations, on ground both of policy and tactics — his support for the approach to Mussolini in May having been a matter of not giving the French the opportunity to recriminate. His position was not so different from Churchill's."[29] But the differences between Halifax and Churchill were not superficial.

◆ ◆ ◆

There were differences between the two men of the Right — between a pragmatist and a visionary, between a Whiggish conservative and a traditionalist reactionary. That "visionary" and "reactionary" (especially the latter) are not necessarily positive adjectives in the English political language is true, but in May 1940, in confronting Hitler, neither pragmatism nor Whiggism would do.

29. Lawlor, *Churchill and the Politics of War,* 75, 60.

The differences between Churchill and Halifax were not merely tactical. Nor were they owing principally to their very different temperaments. According to another British scholar of the period, David Reynolds, Churchill had no plan in May 1940, save the hope that, with the help of the United States, Britain could somehow go on. This was suggested too by Halifax's excellent biographer Andrew Roberts at least by the title of his otherwise mostly unexceptionable chapter about these dramatic days: "Churchill as Micawber," the character in *David Copperfield* who keeps hoping that "something may turn up." But Churchill was no Dickensian character. Nor was he an incarnation of John Bull — not in his personality, in his character, or in his wide interest and knowledge of the world beyond England. To Churchill a "general European settlement" in May 1940, or even any sign of a British inclination to elicit such proposals, would be a deadly danger for British morale. In this Greenwood and Attlee and perhaps Chamberlain too would agree. Unlike Halifax, Churchill was convinced that such a settlement, under *any* conditions, could not be counterbalanced by a maintenance, let alone a guarantee, of British liberty and independence. To him these were not separable issues. Any British acceptance of a German domination of Europe would inevitably mean the reduction of Britain to some kind of a minor partner or even a satellite of Germany. That was, and remained, the essence of Churchill's vision.

From the perspective of retrospect, Churchill was surely right. But that was hardly the end of the matter at the time. One must keep in mind that in May 1940 Churchill's position as prime minister was not as strong as it would become later that summer, and he knew that, too: the tenure of the Belligerent Premier may, after all, be a transitory one. Not that Churchill clung to power for predominantly personal ambitions. A difficult argument, some may say, for isn't every human ambition essentially personal? Still, to employ two figures of speech, he had climbed to the top of the greasy pole (Disraeli's metaphor), but with the purpose of holding up the flag. But: he was not blinded by the breadth of his ambition or by a narrowness of his vision — which is how Hitler believed him to be. He was aware not only of the potential fragility of his power but of that of Britain, too. His knowledge of the former appeared, on more than one occasion, during the three cabinet sessions of that day, when he felt that he should not, because he could not, oppose Halifax's proposals entirely. But he knew that not only was the greasy pole swaying but the flag itself was in danger because of the power of the German storm. If he and Britain were to break, someone other than he would have to hold on to the flag. He thought of Lloyd George. He knew that Lloyd George admired Hitler; he knew that Hitler knew that, too; he knew that Lloyd George thought that Britain had no chance of winning this war against Hitler's Third Reich. Lloyd George was wrong; he was very old,[30] but at least he was not an ideologue; he was someone whom Hitler respected. As early as 13 May Churchill had invited Lloyd George to become a member of the cabinet, as minister of agriculture. Lloyd George refused; he hated Chamberlain. Twice more, in June, Churchill approached Lloyd George and talked to Chamberlain about this. But Lloyd George refused again, mostly because of Chamberlain, and Churchill knew that his loyalty to Chamberlain had to

30. Lloyd George, after meeting Hitler in 1936, called him "the greatest living German." In October 1939 Lloyd George said openly in Parliament that Hitler's peace offer must be considered seriously. Hitler commented in one of his wartime "Table Talks," in 1942, that Churchill's "real opponent was Lloyd George. Unfortunately he is twenty years too old."

prevail. During the crucial days of late May Lloyd George's name did not come up. Yet I could not forego mentioning this matter, if only to indicate that Churchill was indeed aware of Britain being at the edge of the abyss. If worse came to worst, Churchill thought, Lloyd George rather than someone like Mosley.

Years after the war someone asked Churchill which year of his life he would like to relive. "1940," he said, "every time, every time." Yes — and no. There were some moments that he would not have wanted to revisit. On this Sunday, 26 May, two hours after the last cabinet, he dined with Eden, Ironside, and Ismay. He knew that he had to abandon Calais, where the last guns had fallen silent earlier that afternoon. Yet he had to urge Brigadier Nicholson to fight to the very end — all in vain. For once Churchill's legendary appetite was gone. He ate and drank almost nothing. He sat in silence throughout the dinner. Afterward he stood up and told his friends that he felt physically sick. Lord Ismay remembered: "As we rose from the table, he said: 'I feel physically sick.' He has quoted these words in his memoirs but he does not mention how sad he looked when he uttered them."[31] We know that he was thinking of Calais,

---

31. *The Memoirs of Lord Ismay,* 121. See also Lukacs, *The Duel,* 95: "His spirit was not broken, but the prospect of a British Götterdämmerung was before his eyes." "At times of stress, Churchill often recalled some particular quotation that expressed his feelings. On May 26 he asked John Martin [one of his secretaries] to look up for him a passage in George Borrow's prayer for England at Gibraltar. [George Borrow was the wonderfully eccentric English travel writer of the early nineteenth century; his classic book was *The Bible in Spain.*] Martin gave it to Churchill the following day, and, as he later recalled, 'it matched his mood.' The quotation read: 'Fear not the result, for either shall thy end be a majestic and enviable one, or God shall perpetuate thy reign upon the waters'" (Sir John Martin, letter to Martin Gilbert, 24 October 1982, quoted in Gilbert, *Finest Hour,* 406).

but he knew, too, that through three cabinets that day, against Halifax he did not quite have his way.

◆ ◆ ◆

A few hours after the guns had fallen silent at Calais, the order for Operation Dynamo, the evacuation of the British Expeditionary Force fom Dunkirk, was issued. There was no connection between these two events. We have seen that Gort's decision to retreat toward Dunkirk was made days before; so was the order of the Admiralty to collect all available seaworthy craft for an eventual largescale evacuation. Earlier that day Hitler lifted the halt order, though that could not be implemented until a few hours later. From the south the Germans advanced slowly, as yet with little resistance from the French and British units withdrawing into Dunkirk. By next day certain German spearheads were less than five miles from the town. The port was still largely unvexed by German shelling or air bombardment. During the last six or seven hours of Sunday, 26 May, twenty-eight thousand British nonfighting personnel were off the piers, evacuated, sailing for Dover. A promising sign, but only in retrospect. More than 300,000 were still left around Dunkirk. No one, including Churchill, was optimistic about the prospects of their safe withdrawal to England.

Startling, again, in retrospect, is that nothing of the War Cabinet deliberations filtered through to the public. There was no sign of any division in the War Cabinet and no sign of the gravity of the crisis in any of the newspapers — not in the Monday (27 May) editions, nor in the days that followed. Only in the *Daily Express* was there a fair amount of space devoted to the prospect of Italy entering the war, and even there only a short passage about Reynaud's visit to London on Sunday. There was no sense of the crisis in the letters to the editors. There exists no evidence, again, that this was the result of self-censorship or of self-discipline. The influential owners of the

British newspapers were unaware of the gravity of the discussions in the War Cabinet. This is evident from some of their later reminiscences and also from the scattered letters and diaries of other influential British personages, men and women, of the time. (One interesting, if amusing, item: in late May the radio column of the *Times* still printed the times of broadcasts in English from abroad, including Hamburg, Bremen [also Rome and Milan]. In a private letter to the editor, Geoffrey Dawson, Lady Astor complained about this. Soon this kind of information was withdrawn. Until mid-June the *Times* still referred to "Herr Hitler" and "Signor Mussolini.") In both the published and unpublished diaries and letters of Harold Nicolson (by then a junior minister of the government), there is no indication that he knew anything about the Halifax-Churchill division. In a letter to his wife on 22 May he had already written about his and her preparations for suicide if the Germans were to land in England and overrun them: "To think that we should come to this! . . . Anyhow you know I have always seen the possibility of defeat since the beginning of the war and even before that. Darling . . . the dots represent all the things I can't say." At night on 26 May he wrote: "What makes it worse is that the blue-bells are still smoking in the woods and that boys of Cranbrook school have a holiday and are plashing around naked in the lake. . . . I look around the garden feeling I may never see it again." He went on: "It is strange to record the emotions of the last ten days. My own experience is as follows: (a) The first realisation that the Germans had by their superior air and tank power broken through and separated the two armies filled me with despair and fear, (b) I then passed to the conclusion that the next thing would be the invasion of these islands and especially of Kent. (c) I then faced the fact that if that succeeds I should personally be shot and that Vita [his wife] would or might be exposed to persecution. (d) I then saw that I must be prepared to commit suicide. And help Vita do the same. But when I found that she took it so calmly and agreed a great calm descended upon me and I saw that it was really most unlikely that this might occur. I therefore returned [to London, that night] in high spirit. . . . We are not in the least beaten but we must prepare for the worst."[32]

Nicolson's mood seems to have been in accord with that of the British people in general. According to the "Secret" report (summary) of the Ministry of Information, "Public Opinion on the Present Crisis": "Reports show a certain steadiness of morale over the weekend. This is partly due to acceptance of what is believed to be a deliberate policy of restricting news. One gets the impression that opinions are being withheld and emotions held in suspense deliberately. . . . By the withholding of news the public has been given a mandate to delay judgment and not to worry. . . . On the other hand, the continued detailed publication of German claims and communiqués in the press has an effect of cancelling out this relief and detachment." Again the report compared the morale in London with that in the provinces and countryside, where spirits continued to be "noticeably higher": "Reports from the Regions indicate some satisfaction over the development of plans for the mobilisation of man power. 'The whiter the collar the less the assurance' is the report of our Regional Information Officer at Reading." In Newcastle: "19 members of Durham Light Infantry are telling alarming stories of wiping out of a D.L.I. battalion in Boulogne, and confusion among the wounded, etc. at the quayside; the result is some public anxiety and anger." Leeds: " 'We're alright, but people at the top are

32. The first quote is from *Diaries and Letters of Harold Nicolson*, 87–88; the second is from the unpublished excerpts of the diary (typed by Nicolson) in the library of Balliol College.

wrong.'" Reading (southern): "Church attendance up. Bitterness towards Germany increases, thanks to refugee stories. Allied counteroffensive anxiously awaited. Oxford optimistic." Manchester: "Excellent spirit in factories. Rumours still growing. Nicholson's [*sic*] broadcast thought not to have had enough punch." Belfast: "German violation of Eire as a possibility has made people nervous. Division of opinion over Conscription: majority against it for fear of disloyalist section." London: "Suspense: people getting on with their own affairs; some fatalism while waiting for news. . . . Undercurrent of anxiety is present especially among women who realise the sacrifice of life: 'we shall win — but at what price.' Sunday services well attended; some emotionalism displayed. . . . Working-classes . . . listen regularly to Haw Haw at 9.15. Cinema audiences thin. Comedies and musicals preferred to serious and war pictures. New internment of aliens approved. Mistrust of the French expressed."[33]

Most of this is in accord with the Mass-Observation reports of morale as reported on Sunday and Monday.[34] "Intensive investigation carried on over the weekend shows a general levelling up and steadiness in morale, but this is partly at the expense of interest and identification with the events in France. The cut-down of news . . . give people, as it were, an *excuse* for not carrying on with the process of facing up to the facts, a process which has been steadily increasing in recent days. Today in particular, there is noticeable a small, but significant increase in fatalism again, in general interest and quality of opinion. . . . Off setting possible disadvantages arising from this, is the definite advantage that the violent day to day swings and short-time anxiety is automatically relieved for many people by the

33. No. 9, INF 1/264 Monday, 27 May 1940.
34. FR 142, 27.5.40.

slackening of the news tempo. . . . Opinion is that on the whole the news is a little better, although opinion is not very certain of itself."[35]

♦ ♦ ♦

We began this reconstruction of this grave day, 26 May 1940, with an account of the National Day of Prayer in Westminster Abbey. Allow me now to end it with a poem by the gentle English poet John Betjeman. In "In Westminster Abbey" his ironic stanzas portray a somewhat frivolous Englishwoman of a certain class, not of course on that deeply dramatic day of 26 May but most probably earlier, during the Reluctant War.

> Let me take this other glove off
>   As the *vox humana* swells,
> And the beauteous fields of Eden
>   Bask beneath the Abbey bells.
> Here, where England's statesmen lie,
> Listen to a lady's cry.
>
> Gracious Lord, oh bomb the Germans.
>   Spare their women for Thy Sake,
> And if that is not too easy
>   We will pardon Thy Mistake.
> But, gracious Lord, whate'er shall be,
> Don't let anyone bomb me.
>
> Keep our Empire undismembered
>   Guide our Forces by Thy Hand,

35. A footnote in that report: "It may be noted that yesterday gasmask carrying was at the highest noted for many months, 19.6% in the morning, and 20.3% in the afternoon definitely carrying their masks, as compared with e.g. 13.2% on the 16th, and 8.7% on the 17th last week. (Counts taken at standard points and by standard technique.)"

Gallant blacks from far Jamaica,
    Honduras and Togoland;
Protect them Lord in all their fights,
And, even more, protect the whites.

Think of what our Nation stands for,
    Books from Boots' and country lanes,
Free speech, free passes, class distinction,
    Democracy and proper drains.
Lord, put beneath Thy special care
One-eighty-nine Cadogan Square.

Although dear Lord I am a sinner,
    I have done no major crime;
Now I'll come to Evening Service
    Whensoever I have the time.
    So, Lord, reserve for me a crown,
And do not let my shares go down.

I will labour for Thy Kingdom,
    Help our lads to win the war,
Send white feathers to the cowards
    Join the Women's Army Corps,
Then wash the Steps around Thy Throne
In the Eternal Safety Zone.

Now I feel a little better,
    What a treat to hear Thy Word,
Where the bones of leading statesmen.
    Have so often been interr'd.
And now, dear Lord, I cannot wait
Because I have a luncheon date.[36]

---

36. John Betjeman, "In Westminster Abbey," *Collected Poems* (1979).

CHAPTER FIVE

Monday, 27 May

What was happening at Dunkirk. – The Belgians surrender. – American considerations. – Three War Cabinets and a walk in the garden. – "You'd have been better off playing cricket."

In the last days of May 1940 the fate of Britain—indeed, the outcome of the Second World War—depended on two things. One was the division between Churchill and Halifax. The other was the destiny of the British army crowding back into Dunkirk. These two matters were of course connected. But this appears only in retrospect. Churchill said that he would fight even if the BEF were lost ("our greatest military defeat for many centuries"). The final order to begin evacuation, Operation Dynamo, was issued a few minutes before seven o'clock on Sunday, 26 May, and Gort had been pulling back toward Dunkirk for several days before that; but no one thought that anything beyond a fraction of the almost half million British and French troops, now surrounded and squeezed by the Germans, could escape to England. It was not until about 31 May, more than five days later, that the prospect of a truly large-scale evacuation—including many of the French troops in and around Dunkirk—arose. It was certainly not foreseen earlier. This should appear from the first instructions of the Admiralty to Admiral Sir Bertram Ramsey, who was in charge of the operation in Dover: "It is imperative for 'Dynamo' to be implemented with the greatest vigour, with the view of lifting up to 45,000 of the B.E.F. within two days, at the end of which it is probable that evacuation will be terminated by enemy action." These instructions were drafted by Sir Dudley Pound, a notably cautious First Sea Lord; but there was not much reason to think or to estimate otherwise. In the end Dunkirk was not occupied by the Germans until nine days later, and nearly eight times more British and French soldiers were landed in Britain than what Pound had estimated. No one could have predicted this on 26 May, nor indeed for some time thereafter.

We have seen that Hitler had lifted the halt order on 26 May. Later that afternoon the advance of the German units from the south toward Dunkirk began. The siege of Dunkirk (if it can be called that) began in earnest early the next morning, on Monday, the twenty-seventh. At 7:15 A.M. Vice Admiral Somerville woke Churchill with a telephone call. The Germans had advanced their guns north of Calais and had begun to shell ships approaching Dunkirk.

Much worse than this shelling were the German bombs that started to rain on Dunkirk and the troops retreating thereto. In more than one way this day, 27 May, was the worst of the entire Dunkirk saga. The Germans ruled the air, with relatively little interference from the Royal Air Force. This was partly because the chiefs of the air staff had decided to preserve as much of the RAF as possible for the event of a German onslaught on Britain. When British fighters over Dunkirk attacked the slower German bombers they were often successful, but there were not many of them—something that filled the mass of British troops throughout the Dunkirk days and nights with outspoken bitterness and something that Churchill himself had to admit and explain in his speech on 4 June, after Dunkirk. As bad as the bombing raids on Dunkirk, if not worse, were the German dive-bomber attacks on the columns of the British and the French retreating along the dusty roads and lanes toward the town and port. Within the port the first attempts to organize the evacuation of masses of troops were only beginning. Two developments were fortunate that day. One was the achievement of a British officer, Captain W. G. Tennant, in making one of the two main piers of the port of Dunkirk serviceable for landing, loading, and pulling away. The other was the realization of the advantages of the long, sandy beaches north of the town, reachable also by small craft. Yet, all in all, on this shattering twenty-seventh day of May, not more than 7,700 British troops were able to leave for England. Next day there would be 18,000, but that was not much, either. Indeed, the two-day total was far less than the maximum of 45,000 stated by the first sea lord in his initial orders.[1]

It seems that Churchill himself was not quite aware of the situation at Dunkirk on the twenty-sixth — surely not at the beginning of this long day. In a message to Gort the previous night he had said: "At this solemn moment I cannot help sending you my good wishes. No one can tell how it will go. But anything is better than being cooped up and starved out. . . . Presume troops know that they are cutting their way back home to Blighty. Never was there such a spur for fighting. We shall give you all that the Navy and Air Force can

---

1. There is a record of twenty-six thousand noncombatants lifted off from Dunkirk on 26 May: a contemporary guess rather than an accurate figure, since precise statistics begin only on 27 May.

do."[2] "All" was a slight exaggeration. We have seen that a wholesale engagement of the British fighter force in the battle over Dunkirk was not undertaken, and with good reason. The splendid efforts of the navy during the seven days of Dunkirk were decisive for the evacuation; but, save for destroyers and other smaller craft, larger warships and the bulk of the navy stationed farther north in Britain were not thrown into the battle — as indeed there would be no such engagement even in the event of a German cross-Channel invasion later that summer. All historic precedents notwithstanding, the waters of the Channel in 1940 would see nothing like what had happened in 1588 with the Spanish Armada or what could have happened with Bonaparte's armada in 1803: for more than one reason, the bulk of the fleet in 1940 could not be sacrificed.

Meanwhile, at Dunkirk and in the large but steadily shrinking pocket where the BEF was retreating, fierce small skirmishes erupted all day, while the British were systematically destroying their vehicles, stores, ordnance, and other equipment. The French did not understand this. They still thought that the Dunkirk pocket was to be held rather than evacuated. (Also, the brave defense of Lille by the First French Army, led by General Prioux and Molinié, holding out until 1 June, delayed a fair number of German units otherwise ready to push on to Dunkirk.)

It may be asked — it has been asked by a few historians, but not

2. Churchill Papers, CA 20/14. It is dated 27 May, but this must be wrong: the message still speaks of fighting in Calais, and it ends: "Anthony Eden is with me now and joins his good wishes to mine" — surely a reference to their dinner on 26 May. Also, in his dispatch Churchill still suggests a *British* attack southward from the Dunkirk perimeter ("A column directed upon Calais while it is still holding out might have a good chance"); this was both unreasonable and impossible.

until decades after these events — why the German land offensive aimed at Dunkirk was relatively slow. A fierce direct thrust into Dunkirk, if so ordered by Hitler, would have been possible. It would have meant the end, that is, the capture of the entire British Expeditionary Force and perhaps of much else besides. But such a last-ditch battle would have been bitter and bloody. There may have been political calculations, too, in Hitler's mind. Still the decisive element was his inclination to agree with Goering to the effect that, at Dunkirk, Goering's Luftwaffe, that is, German air superiority, could do the job.[3]

So this Monday, 27 May, was a very bad — perhaps the worst — day at Dunkirk and for the entire British Expeditionary Force, whose retreat was now imperiled by another factor, the political consequences of which were even more damaging than its military ones: Belgium, King Leopold III had decided, was to surrender. Churchill knew this; as a matter of fact, he, unlike the French, had a measure of melancholy understanding for the situation of the king who had decided to stay with his people. (The night before, Churchill had written to Gort, "We are asking them to sacrifice themselves to us.") But the Belgian army was falling apart. Churchill knew that the king's decision to remain meant that Leopold saw the war as lost and would ask the Germans for a separate peace. Early on the twenty-seventh, Churchill wrote to Sir Roger Keyes, his personal envoy to the king: "By his present decision the King is dividing the nation and delivering it into Hitler's protection." This was true. "Please convey these considerations to the King and impress on him

3. Goering himself on 27 May: "Only a few fishing boats are coming across; one hopes that the Tommies know how to swim" (cited in Engel, *Heeresadjutant bei Hitler.*)

the disastrous consequences on the Allies and to Belgium."[4] Late that night General Edward Spears telephoned Churchill from Paris with the news that King Leopold had sent a plenipotentiary to the Germans and asked for a cease-fire at midnight.

◆ ◆ ◆

Thus ended this day of disaster across the English Channel. What happened within the War Cabinet in London was not less dramatic.

Or, perhaps, decisive. Churchill knew that. He braced himself for a day that would be as difficult as the day before, if not more so. (It may be interesting that in his otherwise precise household schedule there is no entry for Monday, 27 May.) We have seen that he was awakened by a telephone call from Vice Admiral Somerville as early as 7:15. Then he went through a very large sheaf of papers, mostly dispatches about the military situation, preparing himself for the first War Cabinet meeting, which met in Downing Street at half past eleven.

This was an unusually long meeting, concerning mostly, though not exclusively, military matters, during which Chamberlain, somewhat unusually, spoke at length. The military reports were sometimes confusing and often no longer accurate. The chief of the Imperial General Staff had reported: "Our troops in Calais were still holding out with great gallantry. Some of the garrison had been withdrawn to naval vessels, and were to be replaced by other men of the same unit." This was astonishing: for fighting in Calais had ended more than sixteen hours earlier.

The survey of the situation of the British Expeditionary Force took a long time. Then Chamberlain brought up the question of what should be told to the Dominions. This was a serious matter,

4. CA 20/14.

since the high commissioner for Australia in London, Stanley Bruce, was evidently a defeatist. He had told Chamberlain the night before that he did not think that Britain could continue the war if France fell out, and that Britain had to learn something about possible terms (perhaps through Mussolini). At the War Cabinet, Chamberlain said that he would "see the High Commissioners again, and inform them that even if France went out of the war, there was no prospect of our giving in. We had good reason to believe that we could withstand attack from Germany, and we were resolved to fight on."[5] (Bruce was not convinced and insisted on his gloomy view for several days, after which he faded out of the picture.) The first lord of the Admiralty, A. V. Alexander, a Labourite, was present at this meeting. He knew that Bruce was a defeatist. (So did the Dominions secretary, Viscount Caldecote, a Conservative, who said that the Australian prime minister was not inclined to agree with Bruce.) At this point Churchill entered the discussion. He thought "that it would be as well that he should issue a general injunction to Ministers to use confident language. He was convinced that the bulk of the people of the country would refuse to accept the possibility of defeat." Churchill issued such a stern admonition the next day.

There followed a lengthy discussion about the necessary evacuation of Narvik, in Norway, which British, French, and Polish troops had succeeded in occupying two days before — the only, and much

5. There is a parenthetical addition in the minutes after Chamberlain's unexceptionable statement: "(This statement would apply of course to the immediate situation arising out of the hypothetical collapse of France. It would not mean that if at any time terms were offered they would not be considered on their merits.)" This insertion is not clear. Did "terms" mean terms offered to France or to Britain? Both the typescript and its place in the minute suggest that it was added subsequently by the secretary.

belated, Allied victory on land since the beginning of the war. Then came an even longer discussion about the air war, during which Churchill presented estimates that were somewhat more optimistic than those of the chief of the air staff. Then Churchill once more returned to the larger prospects of France. He speculated that France might become a neutral, in which case "it was not certain that Germany would insist on retaining all the ports in northern France. She might be so anxious to divide France from us that she would offer France very favourable terms of peace."[6] Chamberlain followed with a very reasonable summary analysis of the previous reports ("A Certain Eventuality . . . ") of the chiefs of staff. He began, however, by stating that their report "was based on the assumption that the United States of America would be willing to give us full economic and financial support. This was perhaps not an unjustifiable assumption, but we might not obtain this support in the immediate future."

This was so. Churchill knew it. "The United States," he said, "had given us practically no help in the war and now that they saw how great was the danger, their attitude was that they wanted to keep everything which would help us for their own defence." He knew that President Roosevelt was, as yet, both unable and unwilling to commit the United States to stand by Britain in ways that would be both definite and quick. One of Roosevelt's reasons was, of course, domestic American politics, at a time when neither his

6. This was shrewd foresight, though only partly true. What was true was that twenty-four days later, after the complete collapse of France, Hitler chose to offer terms to France that gave the latter a constrained way out of the war — which was why Sir R. Campbell, then the last British ambassador to France, would call them "diabolically clever." But these terms were of course much harsher than Churchill had imagined on 27 May: the Germans retained the entire Channel and Atlantic coasts of France, with all the French ports there.

unprecedented nomination for a third term nor his victory in the subsequent presidential election was assured. Another, more important reason was Roosevelt's view of the greater issue of the war: if worse came to worst, the British fleet could come over to the Western Hemisphere. Churchill had already warned Roosevelt against this in a somber and important message on 15 May. Five days later, in another message that he at first hesitated to send but then dispatched, Churchill warned Roosevelt that he could not and should not count on the British fleet.

Roosevelt was not yet ready to trust Churchill completely. Nor did he trust Kennedy in London, but he did trust his ambassador in Paris, William C. Bullitt, who, though resolutely anti-Hitler, thought at that time that the British might crack and consider a deal with Germany. We have seen that on 24 May Roosevelt even contacted the Canadian prime minister to discuss "certain possible eventualities which could not possibly be mentioned aloud." Thus Roosevelt recognized the first signs of the "eventuality" that Britain might have to sue for peace, and he reacted to this in his own, frequently devious way. His relationship with Churchill had not yet matured into the one of mutual confidence that it would become later that year. On 25 May Halifax drafted a telegram to Roosevelt that, in accord with Churchill—who presumably thought it both futile and not strong enough—he decided not to send.[7] Thus during

7. The wording of this telegram reflected Halifax's often convoluted and cautious phraseology. It suggested that Roosevelt address Hitler directly: "If you . . . say to Hitler that, while you recognize his right to obtain terms that must necessarily be difficult and distasteful to those whom he defeated, nevertheless terms which intended to destroy the independence of Great Britain and France would at once touch the vital interests of the U.S., and that if such insisted upon, you thought it inevitable that the attempt would

the dramatic last ten days of May there were no direct communications between Churchill and Roosevelt.

During this first War Cabinet on the twenty-seventh, Halifax spoke not much. He did mention a telegram from the British ambassador in Washington, who suggested at least the possibility of offering certain British island bases in the Western Hemisphere in exchange for American support. (Such an idea had already been bruited during the king and queen's visit to the United States the previous summer.) That was not worth discussing now, Churchill said. Halifax also made a comment about sending an economic mission to Washington, but otherwise he said little during this lengthy session, which ended with a further discussion about the air war, about military preparations for a possible invasion of England, and about Ireland.[8]

Cadogan, who was present for part of the session, wrote in his diary: "Cabinet at 11:30 — as gloomy as ever. See very little light anywhere."[9] It is not ascertainable where or with whom Churchill or Halifax took their lunch that day. Then, at 4:30, the War Cabinet met again. This meeting was more restricted than the morning one, with few outside officials present except for Sir Archibald Sinclair, the Liberals' leader, secretary of state for air, and a supporter of Churchill.

---

encounter U.S. resistance, the effect might well be to make him think again. If you felt it in the event contemplated to go further and say that, if he insisted on terms destructive of British independence and therefore prejudicial to position of U.S., U.S.A. would at once give full support to G.B., effect would of course be all the more valuable" (Halifax Papers, A. 410.4.1, cited in Roberts, *The Holy Fox,* 212).

8. CAB 65/7, WM 141.
9. Cadogan, *Diaries,* 290.

We have now arrived at the most crucial of the nine War Cabinet sessions during the three days of 26 and 27 and 28 May — a meeting whose mention, let alone reconstruction, Churchill consciously excluded from his inimitable and detailed *History of the Second World War,* his own *War Memoirs.* It was during this meeting, which was somewhat shorter than the previous one that morning, that Halifax felt compelled to confront Churchill directly. He had challenged Churchill the day before, too, but not in so definite a manner. What came to the fore now were not their minor differences but their veritably opposite convictions about the immediate destiny of their country. Now the slow careful Halifax believed not only that the time had come to express his differences with Churchill; he seems to have believed that there was no time left to waste — indeed, if their differences were irreconcilable, he was thinking of resigning from the government. This is why we must attempt to reconstruct the events of this afternoon in considerable detail.

The session began with a discussion of Halifax's draft memorandum, the "Suggested Approach to Signor Mussolini." Churchill said that it was better for Roosevelt to approach Mussolini than for the British to do so through the French. A key sentence in Churchill's initial statement shows that he foresaw the essence of the French tragedy: "If France collapsed, Germany would probably give her good terms, but would expect the French to have the kind of Ministers who were acceptable to the Germans." That is, instead of France falling back into some kind of neutrality, there would come about a France that had switched to the other side: pro-German and anti-British. Halifax did not entirely disagree; he reported the last cryptic news from the British ambassador in Rome, to the effect that "nothing we could do would be of any value at this stage, so far as Signor Mussolini was concerned." Chamberlain largely agreed: he thought that Mussolini might "play any part in the game," but not until "Paris had been taken." Yet, for the sake of the French — or, rather, to avoid letting them down entirely — "it would be unfortunate if they were to add to this that we had been unwilling even to allow them the chance of negotiations with Italy."

Now Churchill made his first statement opposing any approach to Italy — thus stating his opposition to Halifax's "Suggested Approach" in its entirety. He said that Chamberlain's argument "amounted to this, that nothing would come of the approach, but that it was worth doing to sweeten relations with a falling ally." He then read a telegram that he had received from Reynaud that morning, which at least indirectly implied that more important than the Italian business was "the argument which to [Reynaud's] mind carries most weight. . . . The assistance given by Britain to France at this tragic hour will help to strengthen the alliance of hearts which I [Reynaud] believe to be essential." There Churchill stopped. Sir Archibald Sinclair backed him up: "He was convinced of the futility of an approach to Italy at this time. Being in a tight corner, any weakness on our part would encourage the Germans and the Italians, and it would tend to undermine morale both in this country and in the Dominions. The suggestion that we were prepared to barter away pieces of British territory would have a deplorable effect and would make it difficult for us to continue the desperate struggle that faced us. Nevertheless, he was impressed with the importance of doing all we could to strengthen the hands of the French." Attlee and Greenwood said much the same thing. Greenwood said that he saw "no way of getting France out of her difficulty. . . . If it got out that we had sued for terms at the cost of ceding British territory, the consequences would be terrible. . . . It would be heading for disaster to go any further with these approaches."

Halifax interceded only once, and then somewhat obliquely. He came back to the record of his discussion with Bastianini two days before, "in which he had said that we had always been willing to discuss the questions between our two countries and to endeavour to find solutions satisfactory to both sides. The French were not really proposing to go much further than this, except in the direction of geographical precision, where he was not prepared to accept their views. He doubted whether there was very much force in the argument that we must do nothing which gave an appearance of weakness, since Signor Mussolini would know that President Roosevelt's approach had been prompted by us." This was largely true. But what appeared behind Halifax's argument was his realization that Churchill was about to reject his entire "Suggested Approach" unconditionally.

Right he was: for Churchill now made his decisive statement. Phrases of it have been cited by other historians, but here we should reproduce it in its entirety:

> THE PRIME MINISTER said that he was increasingly oppressed with the futility of the suggested approach to Signor Mussolini, which the latter would certainly regard with contempt. Such an approach would do M. Reynaud far less good than if he made a firm stand. Further, the approach would ruin the integrity of our fighting position in this country. Even if we did not include geographical precision and mentioned no names, everybody would know what we had in mind. Personally he doubted whether France was so willing to give up the struggle as M. Reynaud had represented. Anyway, let us not be dragged down with France. If the French were not prepared to go on with the struggle, let them give up, though he doubted whether they would do so. If this country was beaten, France became a vassal state; but if we won, we might save them. The best help we could give to M. Reynaud was to let him feel that, whatever happened to France, we were going to fight it out to the end.

This manoeuvre was a suggestion to get France out of the difficulty that she might have to make a separate peace, notwithstanding her bargain not to do so.

At the moment our prestige in Europe was very low. The only way we could get it back was by showing the world that Germany had not beaten us. If, after two or three months, we could show that we were still unbeaten, our prestige would return. Even if we were beaten, we should be no worse off than we should be if we were now to abandon the struggle. Let us therefore avoid being dragged down the slippery slope with France. The whole of this manoeuvre was intended to get us so deeply involved in negotiations that we should be unable to turn back. We had gone a long way already in our approach to Italy, but let us not allow M. Reynaud to get us involved in a confused situation. The approach proposed was not only futile, but involved us in a deadly danger.

It is perhaps not unreasonable to assume that by naming Reynaud in the penultimate sentence Churchill also meant Halifax. Chamberlain now injected a calming proposal of compromise: "While he agreed that the proposed approach would not serve any useful purpose, he thought that we ought to go a little further with it, in order to keep the French in a good temper. He thought that our reply should not be a complete refusal." However, let Roosevelt address Mussolini first; this would give Britain some time.

Churchill now made a brief statement about the fighting spirit of the French army; he had heard that morning that there was some improvement there. "Otherwise everything would rest on us. If the worse came to the worst, it would not be a bad thing for this country to go down fighting for the other countries which had been overcome by the Nazi tyranny."

Halifax now had had enough. He began by saying that he largely agreed with Chamberlain. "Nevertheless, he was conscious of certain *rather profound differences of point of view* that he would like to make clear" (my italics).

> He could not recognize any resemblance between the action which he proposed, and the suggestion that we were suing for terms and following a line which would lead us to disaster. In the discussion of the previous day he had asked the Prime Minister whether, if he was satisfied that matters vital to the independence of this country were unaffected, he would be prepared to discuss terms. The Prime Minister had said that he would be thankful to get out of our present difficulties on such terms, provided we retained the essentials and the elements of our vital strength, even at the cost of some cession of territory.

Here was Halifax's attempt to nail Churchill down. He went on:

> On the present occasion, however, the Prime Minister seemed to suggest that under no conditions would we contemplate any course except fighting to a finish. The issue was probably academic, since we were unlikely to receive any offer which would not come up against the fundamental conditions which were essential to us. If, however, it was possible to obtain a settlement which did not impair those conditions, he, for his part, doubted if he would be able to accept the view now put forward by the Prime Minister. The Prime Minister had said that two or three months would show whether we were able to stand up against the air risk. This meant that the future of the country turned on whether the enemy's bombs happened to hit our aircraft factories. He was prepared to take that risk if our independence was at stake; but if it was not at stake he would think it right to accept an offer which would save the country from avoidable disaster.

Churchill said "that he thought the issue which the War Cabinet was called upon to settle was difficult enough without getting involved in the discussion of an issue which was quite unreal and was most unlikely to arise. If Herr Hitler was prepared to make peace on the terms of the restoration of German colonies and the overlordship of Central Europe, that was one thing. But it was quite unlikely that he would make any such offer."

Chamberlain "thought that if concrete proposals were put before the War Cabinet there would be no difficulty in settling what were and what were not essential."

This was a suggestion of compromise between Halifax and Churchill. But Halifax spoke up once more:

> THE FOREIGN SECRETARY said that he would like to put the following question. Suppose the French Army collapsed and Herr Hitler made an offer of peace terms. Suppose the French Government said: "We are unable to deal with an offer made to France alone and you must deal with the Allies together." Suppose Herr Hitler, being anxious to end the war through knowledge of his own internal weaknesses, offered terms to France and England, would the Prime Minister be prepared to discuss them?

What is significant in this discourse is that the "Suggested Approach" involving Mussolini and Italy no longer figures in Halifax's argument. His question was, simply and bluntly, Would Churchill consider *any* peace terms, at *any* time? And now Churchill thought that he could not answer with a definite no: "He would not join France in asking for terms; but if he were told what the terms offered were, he would be prepared to consider them."[10]

10. That was as far as he went. Nearly sixty years later there are different shades of interpretations about this cabinet session. Andrew Roberts, in his

Chamberlain thought that Hitler's tactics would likely be to make a definite offer to France and, when the French responded that they had allies, then he would say, "I am here, let them send a delegate to Paris." "The War Cabinet thought that the answer to such an offer could only be 'No.'"

---

biography of Halifax, writes that the compromise put forward was Churchill's, not Chamberlain's. He is right in saying that when Halifax tried to pin Churchill down, he "took advantage of Churchill's attempt to be as moderate as possible, the better to sell his policy to the War Cabinet, and in particular to carry Chamberlain with him"; "Halifax was angry at the way Churchill twisted and misrepresented his arguments. . . . He was incensed by the way Cabinets, which were designed for sober and mature reflection, had instead to hear harangues in which romanticism and illogicality vied for the upper hand" (*The Holy Fox,* 220–21). There is a slight element of exaggeration in his otherwise balanced judgment. David Dilks, citing Churchill's last statement "that while he would not join France in asking for terms, he would be prepared to consider them if told of them," adds: "Here was Churchill, of all people, prepared to think of a peace which would inevitably leave Germany master of Europe and would also involve the loss of some British territory. The traditional belief that Churchill, from the moment of his accession as Prime Minister, was determined to fight until the whole of Europe was liberated can no longer be sustained in pure form" (Dilks, "The Twilight War and the Fall of France"). This is exaggerated: the issue, certainly at the end of May 1940, was the survival of an independent Britain; moreover, Churchill had never fought for the *whole* of Europe, not in 1940 nor later. I am more inclined to accept the calm and reasoned summary of Philip Bell: "The War Cabinet discussions of 26, 27, and 28 May marked a decisive point in British history, and by implication in the history of Europe. There can be no doubt that if the War Cabinet had agreed to the French proposal, and approached Mussolini with a view to mediation, they would not have gone back on that decision. Once the possibility of negotiation had been opened, it could not have been closed, and the government could not

Very well: but Halifax still insisted that he did not wish to "send a flat refusal" to the French. It was then agreed that Reynaud should get a draft along the lines that had been suggested by Chamberlain. The meeting ended with a brief discussion about the United States and the British fleet: "President Roosevelt seemed to be taking the view that it would be very nice of him to pick up the bits of the British Empire if this country was overrun. It was as well that he should realize that there was another aspect to the question."[11]

But the essential matter was the split in the cabinet. Hadn't Halifax, if somewhat obliquely, suggested that he might resign? And now came the walk in the garden, about which, alas, we have no account either from Halifax or from Churchill. For now Halifax asked Churchill "to come out in the garden with him" for a talk. Before that Halifax told Cadogan, "I can't work with Winston any longer." Cadogan: "I said 'Nonsense: his rhodomontades probably bore you as much as they do me, but don't do anything silly under the stress of that.'"[12] What exactly Churchill told Halifax in the garden we do not know; neither man left a record of their discussion. It

---

have continued to lead the country in outright defiance of German power" (*A Certain Eventuality,* 48).

11. CAB 65/13, WM 142. Early that morning the British ambassador in Washington, Lothian, reported that he had talked with Roosevelt, who, "thinking aloud," repeated his idea that the British navy, in the event of a German victory, should sail to Canada and that the royal family should remove to Bermuda, since "the American republic may be restless at monarchy being based on the American continent" (WM 142, Appendix).

12. Cadogan, *Diaries,* 291. "H. came to have tea in my room after. Said he had spoken to W., who of course had been v. affectionate! I said I hoped he really wouldn't give way to annoyance to which we were all subject and that, before he did anything, he would consult Neville. He said that of course he would and that, as I knew, he wasn't the one to take hasty decisions."

"Halifax [right] told Cadogan, 'I can't work with Winston any longer.'
Cadogan: 'I said "Nonsense: his rhodomontades probably bore you as
much as they do me, but don't do anything silly under the stress of that."'"

is unlikely that Churchill had some kind of secret intelligence information that he could impart only to Halifax. What is more likely is that he was able to charm and soothe Halifax somewhat (he had done this once in the past)[13] but, more important, that he impressed Halifax that his resignation from the government would open up the gravest possible national crisis. Still it is very doubtful that during that brief stroll Churchill was able to convince Halifax of the rightness of his own views.[14]

There was, again, a third War Cabinet that day, at the unusually late hour of ten o'clock. It dealt almost exclusively with the consequences of the Belgian surrender. The minister of information, Duff

13. See above, pp. 65–66.

14. Halifax, who, as we saw, wrote nothing about this episode, still wrote in his diary that night: "I thought Winston talked about the most frightful rot, also Greenwood, and after bearing it for some time I said exactly what I thought of them, adding that, if that was really their view, and if it came to the point, our ways must separate. . . . I despair when [Churchill] works himself up to a passion of emotion when he ought to make his brain think and reason" (Halifax Diary, 27 May 1940). This obviously shows that Halifax was not convinced by Churchill. However, we must consider, too, that his diary was written principally — indeed, exclusively — for his family. It was not a political diary, although it seems that the above was more than an outburst of bitterness; he may have wished to state his position (if that is what it was) with a view to the future. At the same time it may be significant that his own reconstruction ("I said exactly what I thought of them"), including his threat of resignation, does not figure in the War Cabinet record of the session. About this Roberts, *The Holy Fox*, 221, is probably right: "[Halifax's] threat on 27 May had a strong effect on Churchill, who could not afford to see his Government so publicly, swiftly and fundamentally split, especially on what was bound to be publicly perceived as the issue of peace or war. Of course Halifax knew this too, rendering the exercise more of a warning shot than a serious intention to go."

Cooper, "suggested that the public should be given some indication of the serious position in which the B.E.F. had been placed. . . . There was no doubt that the public were, at the moment, quite unprepared for the shock of realisation of the true position." Churchill "thought that the seriousness of the situation should be emphasised, but he would deprecate any detailed statement or attempt to assess the results of the battle, until the situation had been further cleared up. The announcement of the Belgian Armistice would go a long way to prepare the public for bad news."[15]

Before this last session Churchill had received a long dispatch from Spears in Paris, who had had a long talk with Reynaud.[16] Churchill retired at midnight, after having asked for "a very weak" whiskey and soda. His spirits were better than they had been the night before. But his situation was not secure. After two days of protracted and exhausting debates his resolution had not, after all, carried the day.

◆ ◆ ◆

Despite the secrecy of the War Cabinet, for the first time some word of what had happened there filtered out. John Colville wrote in his diary: "There are signs that Halifax is being defeatist. He

15. CAB 65/7, WM 143 (40).

16. "[Reynaud] was, I thought, rather yellow at the gills. . . . He added that he himself would go on to the end, but that he could not disguise the fact that if the Germans really advanced on the Seine others, ready to negotiate, would replace him. . . . I have located the nigger in the fence [*sic*] as far as Reynaud is concerned, the pessimist who, fat and sly, sits next door to him, pouring defeatism in his ears. It is Lt.-Col. de Villelune [*sic*], his private military adviser, in whom he has great confidence. . . . If [Villelume] is half as dishonest and furtive as he looks, he has Fagin beat by furlongs. . . . The French people are not angry yet. They are resolute and calm but bewildered" (PREM 3/188/6).

says our aim can no longer be to crush Germany, but rather to pre-serve our own integrity and independence. Fortunately Ironside is gone."[17] Hugh Dalton wrote in his diary: "After having studied the most important and secret papers, I am told at the Ministry that I am not wanted at the Cabinet this morning as only War Cabinet mem-bers will be there. . . . Some streaks of defeatism are visible in some of the private papers." Dalton saw Attlee briefly after lunch, "Minis-ters and high officials will all get a high directive from the P.M. not to talk or look defeatist."[18] In neither the published nor the un-published diaries of Harold Nicolson is there any indication that he knew about the bitter debate in the War Cabinet.[19]

Nancy Astor (the American-born politician who became the first woman to sit in the House of Commons) wrote in a letter that day, "The news is bad but I am told it is not as bad as it looks."[20] The *Manchester Guardian* of 27 May cited Nicolson's word for

17. Colville, *The Fringes of Power,* 140.

18. *The Second World War Diary of Hugh Dalton,* 23. "On 27 and 28 May Roosevelt learned from Kennedy and from Knox's *Chicago Daily News* bu-reau in London that a part of the Cabinet was talking about the possibility of a negotiated peace" (Reynolds, *The Creation of the Anglo-American Al-liance,* 115). (How did such second-line American newspapermen in Lon-don know something that the British newspaper owners themselves did not know, or of which they were hardly aware?)

19. A rapid note to his wife from his office in the Ministry of Information: "I am afraid that the news this afternoon is very bad indeed, and that we must expect the Germans to surround a large portion of our army and occupy the whole area of Belgium and Northern France. We must also face the possibility that the French may make a separate peace, especially if Italy joins in the conflict. . . . I think you had better keep this to yourself for the moment" (*The Diaries and Letters of Harold Nicolson,* 90).

20. Astor Papers, 1416/1/2.

rumormongers: "chatter-bugs." "We are now suffering from a virulent form of the rumour epidemic." The day before, Duff Cooper had broadcast to France in French. This was reported in the *Times* of 27 May under the headline "German Peace Trap for France," suggesting that at least something of the secret discussions about a possible French withdrawal from the war did filter through. (People often called Duff Cooper's public opinion reporters "Cooper's Snoopers.") The *Daily Express* as well as the *Yorkshire Post* suggested that Mussolini's entry into the war may now have become well-nigh inevitable. The Rome correspondent of the *Daily Telegraph* reported the portents: "The Duce received his military advisers today. Fierce statements on Italian radio. Remains true that 'ordinary Italians' remain most friendly, but afraid they will soon be involved in the war." That same day: "New productions at London theatres this coming week . . . despite the present difficulties."[21] A front-page

21. "The Peaceful Inn," by Dennis Ogden (George Orwell, in his diary on 31 May, called it "the most fearful tripe." The interesting point was that although the play was cast in 1940, it contained no reference, direct or indirect, to the war). Also "Portrait of Helen," by Audrey Lucas, and "The Tempest," with John Gielgud and sets by Oliver Messel, and "Ghosts," by Ibsen. "'Dr. Brent's Household' by Edward Percy, will open at Richmond." In the *Times* of 27 May appears an interesting letter to the editor from Clive Bell (a Bloomsbury personage) from Charleston: "I bought a newspaper described as 'Sports 4th Edition.' It consisted of eight pages, six of which were devoted to horse- and greyhound-racing. . . . If the Government does not stop racing of all sorts for the duration of the war, its demands on the life, labour and property of all citizens will hardly be taken seriously." On the other hand, Harold Nicolson, in his unpublished diary on 24 May, observed: "Up to Leicester where there is a huge dinner of the 1936 Club. I get a very excellent reception and find that their morale is very good. It is not mere complacency since I give them a test question to vote on, namely,

news item in the *Daily Mail* reported that fifteen towns on the southern coast were to be declared "evacuation areas. Children whose parents wish them to be evacuated are to be sent to Midlands and Wales." These towns included Ramsgate, where hotels and boardinghouses "for vacation" were still being advertised in the same paper.

Items about the war were often inaccurate, misleading, or even false. (*News Chronicle:* "Calais Is Definitely in Our Hands." "300 Austrians Mutiny in Norway." "French Hold Upper Hand on Somme." "60,000 Nazi Wounded in Austria." *Daily Herald:* "Allied Troops Are This Morning Firmly Holding the Channel Ports of Calais, Dunkirk, Ostend and Zeebrugge.") Yet the general impression from the press was still that of a somewhat astonishing calm at home. The stock exchange showed no considerable fluctuation (but then neither had the stock exchange of Paris). In Westminster Cathedral Cardinal Arthur Hinsley's sermon was interrupted by a woman who shouted "Peace!" No charges were brought against her.[22] A vignette in the *News Chronicle:* "A man walked last night into a pub near Staines." A cricketer, in white flannels. A red-faced man spoke up: "He ought to be ashamed of himself." "Talking about me?" "As a matter of fact I was. With the war in this state it's no time for cricket." "Well, I'll ask you a question. What did you do this afternoon?" "Read the papers, watched the wireless, and worried myself sick." "You'd have been better off playing cricket." One or two days later, the weary but smiling masses of soldiers in the trains, just back from Dunkirk,

---

'should the Derby be put off?' They voted some 88 per cent in favour of postponement."

22. A letter to the editor of the *News Chronicle* from an A. B. Young, Tunbridge Wells: "Now is the time to bring back Lloyd George and place him in the War Cabinet. His appointment would bring comfort and strength."

could glimpse white-flanneled men playing cricket on the green-swards of Kent, at some distance from the stations of the Southern Railway, where large crowds of Englishmen and women had spontaneously gathered to present tea and lemonade and sandwiches to the troops and cheer them on.

The 26 and 27 May summaries of Mass-Observation, *Morale: Sunday and Monday,* reported that "there is noticeable a small, but significant increase in fatalism again, in general interest and quality of opinion. Absence of news as a deliberate policy, if long continued, is likely to increase this. There are dangers involved." On Sunday, 26 May: "There is, however, an increase in the remarks showing distrust of the papers which is not specifically connected with the official announcement about news." On Monday, 27 May: "Opinion today is still rather confused. People are in a state of suspense, waiting for definite news. There is an undercurrent of anxiety present, although there are as many who say we shall come through all right as there are those who show anxiety. . . . There is a growing section of women who say that they prefer not to think about it, and who deliberately refrain from listening to the wireless." "In Bolton there was an increased reluctance to express an opinion, as in London. In Liverpool, the opinions expressed show a great advance in 'realism' and decline of 'wishful thinking' as compared with some weeks ago." "East Suffolk remains calm as ever, despite extensive military and flooding operations — the latter much to the annoyance of some farmers." "Oxford: Several complaints of the papers' lack of news which on the whole is taken to mean bad news. But everybody is quite confident we shall win in the end. Several favourable comments on the new Government."[23]

The General Morale: Background Situations, issued a few days later,

23. FR 142.

summed up the past week: "Throughout morale investigations in late May, innumerable unconscious tributes to Hitler, and innumerable expressions of an inferiority feeling towards Germany were obtained."[24] A numerical "Ratio of Optimism to Pessimism" (with "optimism an index figure of 1 throughout") showed pessimism increasing after 21 May: 22–24 May, 1.24; 25–27 May, 1.04; rising to 2.17 on 28–30 May; but then declining to .76 on 31 May–2 June, when at last the better news from Dunkirk was coming through.

24. FR 159.

CHAPTER SIX

Tuesday, 28 May

Morale, opinion, and the press. – "We cannot possibly starve the public in this way." – Foreigners and refugees. – Churchill's instructions and the first War Cabinet. – His statement in the Commons. – The second War Cabinet. – Churchill's coup. – He comes through.

Let us now reverse the usual sequence of these chapters, begin-ning rather than ending with a survey of British morale and opinion. Throughout this period information, opinion, and even sentiment customarily lagged behind what was happening, but now there were were some indications of public opinion catching up with the mili-tary situation. Still, except for literally a few men, most people knew nothing about the conflict between Halifax and Churchill in the War Cabinet — that is, about a challenge to Churchill's leadership and to the course that he was setting. This condition worked in Churchill's favor. Of course, public knowledge of a division in the War Cabinet would have affected and even threatened British morale at this cru-cial time. In retrospect, too — and I do not mean only the retrospect of decades, including that provided by the recent availability of cabinet documents to historians — the absence of knowledge about this governmental crisis contributed to the national inclination to believe throughout this period, as well as later that summer and during the Battle of Britain, that ever since Churchill's assumption of the prime ministership on 10 May his leadership of the nation was not only popular but unquestionable and unquestioned. Charles de Gaulle would admire Churchill's ability "pour remuer la lourde pâte anglaise," his capacity "to stir up the heavy English dough": a fine Gallic phrase, referring to the power of Churchill's speeches — but in June and July.

The people did not know what was "really" happening at Dunkirk. But by 28 May the first news about the possibility of the loss of the entire British Expeditionary Force was beginning to surface — at the very time when the tide at Dunkirk, in the direction of a more or less successful mass evacuation, was about to turn. There was, then, still a time lag; Margery Allingham recalled that day, about the desertion of the Belgian king: "Of all the blows in the wind, and there have been many, this I think was the most sudden and annihilating." And: "Hard on the heels of Belgium came the news of Dunkirk."[1] This corresponds with the Mass-Observation report of 28 May — "all observers agree that the [Belgian] news had given people a great shock, and really shaken them up" — but "the general impression is not on the whole pessimistic, and people are still saying widely that we will pull through in the end."[2]

The general *Morale Survey* reported "a new feature . . . that many

1. Allingham, *The Oaken Heart,* 188, 189.

2. FR 159. However, this does not accord with the retrospective report (above, p. 161) to the effect that the pessimism to optimism ratio was highest during the dates 28 to 30 May.

people who, while making confident or other remarks, use phrases and metaphors which imply a considerable uncertainty or an admiration for Hitler's tremendous abilities. . . . For many [women] he has become a secret and somewhat mystical astrological figure. Whatever he said he would do, he would do it. Low's cartoon in the *Evening Standard* [of 30 May, presumably drawn one or two days before], showing Hitler in a charabanc looking across the Channel, and on the side of the machine LONDON AUGUST 18, on the back a list of other capitals and dates, each successfully ticked. Apparently intended to make Hitler look ridiculous, the unconscious effect on ordinary people was precisely the opposite."[3] Yet more important: "We do not think that people are *essentially* or positively apathetic. They are merely negatively apathetic, because they do not know what they ought to do or how they ought to do it and under the new Churchill leadership they still fail in many respects to conform with what might well be regarded and easily framed as minimum requirements for civilian knowledge and co-operation — e.g. knowledge of how to deal with an incendiary bomb, in its earliest stage. . . . There is a tendency among, for instance, people in the Ministry of Information to think that because the Government is changed, because there is a lively Minister and a lively Parliamentary Secretary, therefore, that the mass of people have been changed too." Yet there was positive comment in the *Morale Today* report of 28–29 May about Minister of Information Duff Cooper's radio speech of the twenty-

3. FR 159. However, an earlier and eventually famous Low cartoon, "All Behind You, Winston" (showing a grim and resolute Churchill, with rolled-up sleeves and clenched fist, marching in front of a great crowd of people doing the same, including Chamberlain and Halifax), had had a considerable effect: Dalton mentioned it to Churchill, who reacted with obvious pleasure at the end of the Outer Cabinet meeting on 28 May.

eighth: "Generally well received, and about half of the people had listened to it. Most were grateful for his frank statement of facts, and were impressed by his confident manner. General opinion was that he spoke the truth, grave though it was, and generally gave his listeners more confidence thereby. . . . Each time, a sympathetic and intelligent liking for his broadcasts had become more marked, and people are beginning almost to rely on him to tell them how the situation should be looked at. In this connection it is, of course, imperative that under no circumstances would he in any way 'let them down,' in the future, as so many leaders have done in the past."[4]

The analysis in the *Morale Today* report of 29 May is so detailed and intelligent about the complexities of public opinion that it may be worth quoting some of it in detail. "Opinion is still very much in a state of shock as a result of the news of the Belgian surrender. Morale is, however, on the whole good. People are if anything *calmer*. There is no very great personal anxiety of invasion fear at the moment, but concern for the B.E.F. is growing as the realisation of the real situation grows."

As the Belgian news came through in the early afternoon a tremendous shock was received. But even so the full realisation of the situation was not borne in on many people. In particular they were protected against facing the full facts by rather confusing broadcast and press statements to the effect that the Belgian Government had decided to carry on with its own army, etc., etc. . . . People continued to believe this partly because many of them do not completely understand any news or news bulletin, and partly because they *wanted* to believe this. . . .

This non-realisation is of course characteristic of every unpleasant impact on the mass of the population.

4. FR 155.

A cartoon from *Punch:* "Meanwhile, in Britain, the entire population, faced by the threat of invasion, has been flung into a state of complete panic."

The subsequent analysis reported that "better off and better edu- cated" people were, on the whole, more pessimistic, if only because of their knowledge of geography across the Channel. At the same time the Belgian surrender brought out expressions of "some wild recrimination" against the Belgian king and even, in one or two instances, against America, mostly among the less-educated classes. "As a result, the implications of the position are not as yet fully realised. Yesterday, concern for the B.E.F. was vague and personal. Today there is a growing realisation that the B.E.F. might be forced to surrender if things came to the worst. In some cases this is felt acutely."

Tuesday, 28 May, was the first instance of such a widespread realization. And yet: "There is an unusual lack of real worry as yet today. A strong section still openly express complete confidence, though in the past few days talk about the *inevitability* of our victory as a walkover has steadily declined. This does not mean that people are not taking the situation seriously, but rather that it had not yet fully sunk in, and the tendency to more stable opinion (due to good leadership) noticed during the last day or two has caused people to hold themselves in check."

The overall accuracy of these reports and assessments of public opinion and popular sentiment generally accord with whatever records we have of personal recollections of the diaries of that day.[5] By coincidence, George Orwell began to keep a war diary on this very day, 28 May: "This is the first day on which newspaper posters are definitely discontinued. . . . Nevertheless of the early *Star*'s eight pages, six are devoted to racing. . . . I hope the B.E.F. is cut to pieces sooner than capitulate. People talk a little more of the war, but very little. As always hitherto, it is impossible to overhear any comments on it in pubs etc. Last night E [Eileen, his wife] and I went to the pub to hear the 9 o'clock news. The barmaid was not going to have turned it on if we had not asked her, and to all appearances nobody listened."[6]

Orwell did not attribute this self-conscious reserve either to stupidity or to torpor. Two days later he wrote: "It is seemingly impossible for them to grasp that they are in danger, although there is

5. About the distinctions of public opinion from popular sentiment see above, p. 29. No such distinctions among these obviously overlapping though still different phenomena appear in the Mass-Observation and Ministry of Information reports. Their usage of the term "public opinion" includes their registrations of popular sentiment.

6. He continued this diary until 28 August 1941 and resumed it again from 14 March to 15 November 1942.

good reason to think that the invasion of England may be attempted in a few days, and all the papers are saying this. [Cyril] Connolly says they will then panic, but I don't think so."[7]

On 28 May Evelyn Waugh took a day off from his post and went to London: "Arriving there I found the news of Belgian surrender on the streets together with women selling flags for 'Animal Day.' . . . Went to Ministry of Information where Graham Greene propounded a scheme for official writers to the Forces and himself wanted to become a Marine. . . . I said the official writer racket might be convenient if we found ourselves permanently in a defensive role in the Far East, or if I were incapacitated and set to training. Returned to find the camp in great despondency. The Commanding Officer went to Aldershot and was told to prepare the troops for the blackest news of the BEF and to keep up their morale."[8] Harold Nicolson's policy committee met in the morning to discuss the Belgian news: "From the purely cynical point of breaking the news to the British public this is not so bad a thing. It will at least enable them to feel that the disaster was due to Belgian cowardice as indeed to some extent it was." Later that evening Nicolson had to make a statement in the House of Commons about the Ministry of Information's budget estimates: "It is a strange feeling to stand at the box which Gladstone struck. I am not nervous in the least and barely conscious of anything but the job in hand, but were it not for this dull pain of war, I should have regarded it as a great moment in my life."[9]

The previous night Nicolson had agreed that the whole system of war communiqués "must be altered and that we cannot possibly

7. In *Collected Essays, Journalism, and Letters of George Orwell,* 340–41, 342.

8. *The Diaries of Evelyn Waugh,* 470–71.

9. Diary, unpublished, in Balliol College, 46.

starve the public in this way." On 28 and 29 May this showed some results: *some* of the war reportage in the newspapers became less absurd. Still, much of the news was misleading or strange. On the opinion page of the *Daily Express* of 28 May appeared "serious news": "The news is grave. It grows graver every hour. There can be no pretence about the serious position of the B.E.F. in Belgium, and the French and Belgian troops with them." (This *after* the Belgian surrender.) Yet the leading article in the *Daily Mail* was titled "Faith in Weygand": "We still wait for Weygand. We await the moment for counter-attack." Six days after the last feeble attempt of anything like a counterattack, this made no sense at all. A headline in the *Daily Mirror:* "3 RAF Aces Bag 100" (?).

One of the strangest tendencies was an encouragement of optimism about Russia—evident, independently from one another, in items in at least three newspapers. (This had a precedent in 1914, when Britain was swept by rumors about troops of their ally Russia arriving in England: people were supposed to have seen some of them with snow on their boots.) It was Halifax's idea to accord with Sir Stafford Cripps's wishes and name him ambassador to the Soviet Union (a disastrous choice, but that would not become evident until much later).[10] The *Daily Mirror* on 28 May printed editorials optimistic about Russia: "We have nothing to lose and everything to gain by a trade agreement and a pact of friendship with the Soviet Union." In the *News Chronicle:* "Russia is certainly showing no desire at the moment to help Hitler wage his war." This was incorrect; it showed the kind of wishful thinking (and wishful writing) that would be characteristic of at least a section of the British press after

10. These two men, on the opposite ends of the political spectrum, were bound by their personal sympathies: Cripps, like Halifax, was a religious puritan of sorts—dyspeptic, ascetic in his habits, and a Yorkshireman.

Hitler's invasion of Russia and thereafter. On the same day the *Manchester Guardian* printed yet another cartoon by Low: Stalin listening carefully but willingly to Cripps, who appears as a British salesman, knocking and opening the Kremlin door — another instance of very wishful thinking. (Soon V. M. Molotov, on Stalin's orders, would congratulate Hitler on the occasion of the German triumph over France.)

In the same *Manchester Guardian:* "Blackburn Mills combing, spinning and weaving yesterday at 6 A.M., instead of 7:45. . . . The working week is now one of 55½ hours." "Weavers at Messrs. Taylor at Hartley's Industrial Mills at Westburton, near Bolton, have refused to work with a conscientious objector (even though he volunteered for A.R.P. Service)." There was a considerable evidence of suspicion of aliens, too. In the *News Chronicle,* 28 May: "Finchley Council decided last night to dismiss the 40 aliens in Finchley civil defense." In the *Daily Mail*'s "Mail Bag": "Hundreds of readers write demanding 'much more stringent treatment of aliens.'" Yet at the same time the Amateur Boxing Association cancelled that year's championship at Wembley Pool, "now a refugee centre." And in the *News Chronicle,* "Answer to Hitler: The Care of Polish Refugee Children in England." And now an (Edwardian) period piece: "Lady Dudley's Escape."[11]

◆ ◆ ◆

It is at this time that a brief, and necessarily incomplete, survey about the contemporary impressions of foreign observers, including refugees, may be warranted. These impressions cannot, of course, be

11. "One of the last persons to get on board ship when Boulogne was evacuated under fire was the Dowager Lady Dudley, known to so many of your elder readers as Miss Gertie Miller of the Gaiety. Lady was at her villa at Le Touquet [so was Wodehouse] where she usually spends the spring. Her

pinpointed to the day of 28 May; they involve, rather, their reactions to the British atmosphere during the last week of May; my rapid survey of the published dispatches, memoirs, and other papers of foreign ambassadors and ministers are gleaned from that period. They were better informed than were foreign newspapermen stationed in London; the reports of the journalists of that time are not particularly interesting. We must keep in mind that the impressions of such highly placed observers are often valuable (a practice that goes back to the instructions and achievements of the ambassadors of the Venetian Republic in the sixteenth century, who were told that their thoughtful observations and their gathering of all kinds of information might be even more important than their practices of negotiations).

Generally speaking, most ambassadors and ministers posted in London were Anglophiles; many of them were sympathetic to the new Churchill government. The exception, as we have seen, was Joseph P. Kennedy, the American ambassador (a disastrous appointment by Roosevelt, who had thought that this posting of an Irish-American politician to London was a political masterpiece). So much has been written about Kennedy since then that it is easy to

---

first appearance on the stage was as the girl babe in the pantomime at the St. James's Theatre Manchester, in 1892." Compare this with the episode recounted by Orwell on 30 May: "Connolly related that recently a ship was coming away from northern France with refugees on board and a few ordinary passengers. The refugees were mostly children who were in a terrible state having been machine-gunned, etc. Among the passengers was Lady — who tried to push herself to the head of the queue to get on the boat, and when ordered back said indignantly, 'Do you know who I am?' The steward answered, 'I don't care who you are, you bloody bitch. You can take your turn in the queue.' Interesting if true" (*Collected Essays, Journalism, and Letters of George Orwell*, 2:341).

sum up his inclinations. He hated Churchill; he thought that the structure of the British Empire and of British society was hopelessly antiquated; he believed that National Socialism and Fascism, and Germany and Italy, were much preferable to Communism and Russia, indeed were probable bulwarks against Russia. In sum, in May 1940 (and for some time thereafter), Kennedy was a defeatist; but then Roosevelt (as well as Halifax and the Foreign Office) knew that, which is why Kennedy's personal messages to Roosevelt were without much effect.[12] The French ambassador, Charles Corbin, was deeply pessimistic, aware of the fraying ties between London and Paris; his dispatches to his government were entirely preoccupied by that matter and give few clues to his views about British morale and opinion.[13] The Italian, Bastianini, was torn — or, rather, was navigating carefully — between his long-standing loyalty to Mussolini and his sympathy for what Halifax was attempting, but by 28 May he

12. However, Churchill and Roosevelt were aware of Kennedy's potential political influence, which is why they continued to transmit their correspondence through the American embassy in London, occasionally spicing them with a few positive phrases about Kennedy. They wished to avoid letting him feel that they were bypassing him because they distrusted him. But, as the summer went on, Kennedy knew that he was being bypassed, and he complained bitterly to Roosevelt. In October he returned to the United States and then resigned.

13. One member of his staff, the diplomat and writer Paul Morand, who had been posted there because of his impeccable knowledge of English and English things, had a low estimate of the British ability to resist and survive. This very cultured and originally very Anglophile personage had gradually become deeply disillusioned in the 1930s by what he saw as a decline, if not a degeneration, of earlier British virtues and qualities. After the French armistice he joined the Pétain regime, ending up as the Vichyite minister to Romania.

knew that the decision for war had been made in Rome. Even so, his dispatch to Rome three days later gave a perceptive account of British morale: for the first time in a week, it was definitely "up."[14] The Soviet ambassador, Ivan Maisky, was a sly personage who had for some time cultivated his relations with Churchill and the Churchillians, an approach that the latter rather unjustifiably attributed to pro-British inclinations—none of which appears in his dispatches sent to the Kremlin at the time. Franco's ambassador to the Court of St. James's was the Duke of Alba, an aristocrat descended from ancient British bloodlines. In May 1940 Alba's sympathies for Churchill were not yet evident, but in his case, unlike those of some other Spanish diplomats of that period, sympathies for Germany were entirely absent. At the end of May the Danish and Belgian ministers were in a very difficult position, the former still representing a government now under German control, the latter (Cartier de Marchienne, an antique diplomatist from another age), in a most frightful dilemma between loyalty to his king and loyalty to the Belgian government, which had fled to France and was denouncing the king's capitulation. The Polish minister, Count Edward Raczynski, was splendidly resolute. Among the neutrals the ministers of Sweden (Björn Prytz) and of Hungary (György Barcza) not only were Anglophiles but were much impressed by Churchill, and—as were other foreign observers, too—by the discipline and patriotism of the people, including the upper classes, who during the last ten days of May seemed to have accepted drastic restriction of their personal liberties and even more drastic governmental confiscations of many of their foreign assets and investments and much of their taxable income, all without a murmur.

In these last days of May 1940 Britain harbored more than 100,000

14. *Documenti diplomatici italiani*, series 9, vol. 4, 522.

refugees, while more of them were still arriving from France. We have seen that there was considerable popular distrust of aliens. This, together with the prevalent anxiety about possible spies and so-called fifth columnists, contributed to the government's decision to corral refugees who had come from Germany, Austria, and Czechoslovakia, interning them on the Isle of Man. This was not done for the recently arrived and currently arriving refugees from Holland, Belgium, and now from France: the French soldiers evacuated from Dunkirk were generously treated by both government and population. One of these, the fine French historian Marc Bloch, one of the first coming from Dunkirk, was much impressed by the calm and resolute discipline of the British, especially in contrast to the confusion and irresolution of French officials whom he encountered a few days later when he shipped back to France to continue in the war. The scattered reminiscences of Central European refugees, many of them Jewish, tell us little about their impressions of Britain in May 1940: they were fearful about their own future, naturally enough, and the stolidity of their hosts at times confused and distressed them. As in most other cases, their reminiscences of Britain later that summer and during the Blitz are more telling, and sometimes inspiring.

◆ ◆ ◆

Those with some information on this day, 28 May, were still pessimistic about Dunkirk. Alexander Cadogan was present at the War Cabinet that morning. Later that day he wrote in his diary: "Prospects of the B.E.F. blacker than ever. Awful days!"[15] General Pownall, Gort's chief of staff, had some interesting thoughts about the relative caution of the Germans: "It is true that we have not had to bear the same weight or attack that was brought to bear on the others, And is it entirely by accident that the German *stops* when he

15. Cadogan, *Diaries,* 291.

meets us and tries to get success elsewhere, where there may be a gap, or a place defended by one or other of our allies?"[16] Four years later Pownall felt compelled to write: "I shall not ever forget my feelings during the black fortnight in May, 1940, when the capture or annihilation of the entire B.E.F. seemed almost inevitable. I do not yet know how that came to be avoided."[17]

Churchill himself did not think that more than fifty thousand could be lifted from Dunkirk. That morning he drafted a stern directive, marked "Strictly Confidential": "In these dark days the Prime Minister would be grateful if all his colleagues in the Government, as well as important officials, would maintain a high morale in their circles; not minimising the gravity of events, but showing confidence in our ability and inflexible resolve to continue the war till we have broken the will of the enemy to bring all Europe under his domination. No tolerance should be given to the idea that France will make a separate peace; but whatever may happen on the Continent, we cannot doubt our duty, and we shall certainly use all our power to defend the Island, the Empire, and our Cause."[18] Churchill also minuted to General Ismay early that morning. Among other things he wrote: "If France is still our ally after an Italian declaration of war, it would appear extremely desirable that the combined Fleets, acting from opposite ends of the Mediterranean, should pursue an active offensive against Italy. . . . The purely defensive strategy contemplated by the Commander-in-Chief Mediterranean [Andrew Browne Cunningham] ought not be accepted. . . . Risks must be run at this juncture in all theatres. I presume that the Admiralty have a plan in the event of France becoming neutral."[19]

16. Pownall, *Diaries* 1:352.
17. He wrote this on 1 April 1944, in faraway Burma (ibid. 2:158).
18. Churchill, *Their Finest Hour,* 91–92.
19. CA 20/13.

"Churchill himself did not think that more than fifty thousand could be lifted from Dunkirk . . . " The BEF arrives home, a throng of helmeted men joining the many thousands more returning to England.

We have no evidence that his enemy Hitler knew anything about the difficulty with Halifax in the War Cabinet, but Hitler still thought and hoped that the British would see the light, as he put it. That morning an important dispatch from the British ambassador to Japan, Sir Robert Craigie, was shown to the War Cabinet. The previous day he had met the Japanese foreign minister at lunch, who had asked Craigie "for a private talk": "He enquired whether I do not think that Germany would soon make further peace proposals. . . . I think [the Japanese minister] asked for our talk particularly to convey above information, which must have reached him from some German source. I should like to encourage him in such confidences," wrote Craigie. "I did not, however, like to question him too closely as [to the] nature of actual proposals for fear of encouraging belief that we might be prepared to listen to them."[20]

The War Cabinet met at half past eleven. Most of the business dealt with the Belgian surrender. (Unlike the French and most of the British press, Churchill was not sharp in condemning King Leopold: "No doubt history would criticise the King for having involved us and the French in Belgium's ruin. But it was not for us to pass judgment on him.") Duff Cooper, the minister of information, then pressed "for a frank statement of the desperate situation of the British Expeditionary Force. He feared that, unless this was given out, public confidence would be badly shaken and the civil population would not be ready to accept the assurances of the Government of our ultimate victory." Churchill said that that afternoon he would make a statement in the House of Commons about what was happening in and around Dunkirk. But, he added, "it would be idle to try to forecast the success of this operation at this stage."[21]

Then — and this is significant — Churchill had a private talk with Chamberlain. He asked Chamberlain whether he would agree to invite Lloyd George into the government. Both of them knew that Lloyd George was, to put it simply, defeatist; that a few years before he had spoken of Hitler in the most admiring terms; and that only a

20. FO 371/24407.
21. CAB 65/7, WM 144.

few months earlier he had said openly in Parliament that Hitler's peace offers must be considered seriously.[22] Both also knew that Lloyd George hated Chamberlain — which was why, out of loyalty, Churchill had to consult Chamberlain. This was the second time that Churchill had written to Lloyd George. (We have seen that as early as 13 May he had offered him the post of minister of agriculture.) Now Churchill wrote him again, but laying down the condition that the War Cabinet, including Chamberlain, must be unanimous in such an invitation. The letter was sent the next day.[23] Lloyd George refused the offer. He would not work with Chamberlain. Of course Churchill's main purpose was not only the strengthening of national confidence but also that of national unity. But there was also another matter behind this: if worse came to worst, . . . And would worse come to worst? Churchill was statesman enough to think about that too.

He went back to Admiralty House, where he had a brief lunch. He had prepared a brief statement to make in the House of Commons. He had not appeared there for a week, but he thought that such a statement about the war situation must now be made. He told the members the details of the Belgian capitulation. Again he chose (after some deliberation) not to attack the Belgian king: "I have no intention of suggesting to the House that we should attempt at this moment to pass judgment upon [him]." But the

22. After meeting Hitler in 1936 he compared *Mein Kampf* to the Magna Carta and called Hitler "the resurrection and the way" for Germany (Roberts, *The Holy Fox,* 69).

23. Lloyd George's papers in the Library of the House of Lords, G/4/5/48. In June, Lloyd George said to his secretary that he was "not going with this gang. There will be a change. The country does not realize the peril it is in." On 6 June Churchill tried again, after having consulted Chamberlain as well as Halifax. But Lloyd George again refused.

Belgian government, after fleeing to France, had disassociated itself from the king and proclaimed its continuation in the war. About that, Churchill said, "whatever our feelings may be upon the facts so far as they are known to us, we must remember that the sense of brotherhood between the many peoples who have fallen into the power of the aggressor, and those who still confront him, will play a part in better days than those through which we are passing." Then he turned to what everyone was concerned with, the British at Dunkirk: "The troops are in good heart, and are fighting with the utmost discipline and tenacity, and I shall, of course, abstain from giving any particulars of what, with the powerful assistance of the Royal Navy and the Royal Air Force, they are doing or hope to do. I expect to make a statement to the House on the general position when the result of the intense struggle now going on can be known and measured. This will not, perhaps, be until the beginning of next week." (That was so: his next appearance in the House was on 4 June, after the close of the Dunkirk chapter. It was the second of his most memorable speeches, with the stirring passage that began, "We shall fight on the beaches . . . ") Now he ended with a fine Churchillian fillip:

Meanwhile the House should prepare itself for hard and heavy tidings. I have only to add that nothing which may happen in this battle can in any way relieve us of our duty to defend the world cause to which we have vowed ourselves; nor should it destroy our confidence in our power to make our way, as on former occasions in our history, through disaster and through grief to the ultimate defeat of our enemies.

Churchill's speech was relatively brief. There were only two comments, one by a Labour member, H. B. Lees-Smith: "As he is to make a further statement next week this is not the time for any discussion at all. I will, therefore, confine myself to a single observation. Whatever he may have to tell us in the next few days or weeks or months, we have not yet touched the fringe of the resolution of this country." The other comment was made by Sir Percy Harris, a Liberal: "All I want to say is that the dignified statement of the Prime Minister reflects not only the feeling of the whole House but the feeling of the whole nation."[24] Fine words, and not without substance; yet, concerning the phrase "the feeling of the whole House," it is perhaps of interest that no Conservative members chose to speak. In any event, Churchill was heartened by what the Labour member had said: "We have not yet touched the fringe of the resolution of this country."

But was this "not the time for any discussion" at all? Not in the House, surely; but there was the War Cabinet and Halifax. Churchill had asked the War Cabinet to meet in one of the rooms of the House of Commons, for convenience's sake, he said. This was undoubtedly so, but he also had something else in mind. Thither he now went, where the War Cabinet session opened at four o'clock. Then and there the battle between Halifax and Churchill broke out anew.

> The Foreign Secretary said that Sir Robert Vansittart[25] had now discovered what the Italian Embassy had in mind, namely, that we should give a clear indication that we should like to see mediation by Italy.
>
> The Prime Minister said that it was clear that the French

24. Hansard, 28 May 1940.

25. Bringing up Vansittart's name may have been a calculation on Halifax's part. It is true that Vansittart had had good relations with the Italians, going back well before 1940. At the same time he was known as being extremely anti-German.

purpose was to see Signor Mussolini acting as intermediary between ourselves and Herr Hitler. He was determined not to get into this position.

The Foreign Secretary said that the proposal which had been discussed with M. Reynaud on Sunday had been as follows: that we should say that we were prepared to fight to the death for our independence, but that, provided this could be secured, there were certain concessions that we were prepared to make to Italy.

The Prime Minister thought that the French were trying to get us on to the slippery slope. The position would be entirely different when Germany had made an unsuccessful attempt to invade this country. . . .

The Foreign Secretary said that we must not ignore the fact that we might get better terms before France went out of the war and our aircraft factories were bombed, than we might get in three months' time.

The various possibilities now under development of countering night-bombing were referred to.

The Prime Minister then read out a draft which expressed his views. To him the essential point was that M. Reynaud wanted to get us to the Conference table with Herr Hitler. If we once got to the table, we should then find that the terms offered us touched our independence and integrity. When, at this point, we got up to leave the Conference-table, we should find that all the forces of resolution which were now at our disposal would have vanished. M. Reynaud had said that if he could save the independence of France, he would continue the fight. It was clear, therefore, that M. Reynaud's aim was to end the war.[26]

26. This was neither "clear" nor fair to Reynaud.

The Foreign Secretary said that M. Reynaud also wanted the Allies to address an appeal to the President of the United States.

The Prime Minister thought that a paragraph might be added to the draft outlined by the Lord President [Chamberlain] to the effect that we were ready in principle to associate ourselves with such an appeal.

The Minister without Portfolio [Greenwood] thought that M. Reynaud was too much inclined to hawk around appeals. This was another attempt to run out.

The Prime Minister said that he came back to the point that the French wanted to get out of the war, but did not want to break their Treaty obligations to us. Signor Mussolini, if he came in as mediator, would take his whack out of us. It was impossible to imagine that Herr Hitler would be so foolish as to let us continue our re-armament. In effect, his terms would put us completely at his mercy. We should get no worse terms if we went on fighting, even if we were beaten, than were open to us now. If, however, we continued the war and Germany attacked us, no doubt we would suffer some damage, but they would also suffer severe losses. Their oil supplies might be reduced. A time might come when we felt that we had to put an end to the struggle, but the terms would not then be more mortal than those offered to us now.

The Foreign Secretary said that he still did not see what there was in the French suggestion of trying out the possibilities of mediation which the Prime Minister felt so wrong.

The Lord President [Chamberlain] said that, on a dispassionate survey, it was right to remember that the alternative to fighting on nevertheless involved a considerable gamble. The War Cabinet agreed that this was a true statement of the case.

The Prime Minister said that the nations which went down

fighting rose again, but those which surrendered tamely were finished.

The Minister without Portfolio [Greenwood] said that any course which we took was attended by great danger. The line of resistance was certainly a gamble, but he did not feel that this was a time for ultimate capitulation.

The Foreign Secretary said that nothing in his suggestion could even remotely be described as ultimate capitulation.

The Prime Minister thought that the chances of decent terms being offered to us at the present were a thousand to one against.[27]

It was now five o'clock. It was at this moment that Churchill resorted to what some have called his coup. He asked the War Cabinet to adjourn momentarily and to resume their meeting at seven. He had arranged to address the members of the entire cabinet (the Outer Cabinet as contrasted with the five men of the War Cabinet). This took place in his room in the House of Commons. It took about an hour. Churchill's resolution impressed and swayed all of them. We have seen his own account and Hugh Dalton's account of this in the first pages of this book. The decisive matter in Churchill's peroration came at the end. Churchill admitted (if that is the proper verb) that he had been thinking about whether it "was his duty to consider negotiations" with Hitler. But, he had concluded, "it was idle to think that, if we tried to make peace now, we should get better terms from Germany than if we went on and fought it out. The Germans would demand our fleet — that would be called 'disarmament' — our naval bases, and much else. We should become a slave state, though a British government which would be Hitler's puppet would be set up — 'under Mosley or some such person.' And

27. CAB 65/13, WM 145.

where should we be at the end of all that?" Herbert Morrison, a Labour minister, "asked about evacuation of the Government, and hoped that it would not be hurried. The PM said Certainly not, he was all against evacuation unless things really became utterly impossible in London, 'but mere bombing will not make us go.' "[28]

There are two considerations that argue against the interpretation crediting Churchill for having prepared a coup by such a gathering of his longtime supporters. It was proper for him to speak to the entire cabinet at the time, having not met with most of them for more than a week. More important is the fact that the Outer Cabinet consisted of twenty-nine or thirty ministers of whom at least a dozen (if not more) were Conservatives, inherited from the previous Chamberlain government. New members of the cabinet, and Churchillians, amounted to no more than another dozen. Yet, as Dalton recalled, "No one expressed even the faintest flicker of dissent." We do not know who exactly or how many went up to Churchill at the end of the meeting, patting him on the back. It did not matter. Churchill was more than encouraged; he now knew that he would have his way.

Less than an hour after the other ministers dispersed, Churchill

28. Dalton Diary; see Chapter 1. We have one other account of what Churchill said, in the diary of Leo Amery: "Winston told us the whole story very clearly and dramatically in no way minimising the extent of the disaster or of further disasters which might follow such as a successful march on Paris or a French surrender." (In an added handwritten footnote by Amery: "He told us he did not expect to get more than 50,000 away from Dunkirk.") "One thing he was clear about was that there could be no greater folly than to try at the moment to offer concessions to either Italy or Germany, the powers which were out to destroy us. There was nothing to be done at any rate until we have turned the tide, except fight all out" (Amery, *The Empire at Bay*, 619).

returned to the War Cabinet. This last meeting opened at seven. It was a brief session. Churchill told them what had just happened with the other ministers: "They had not expressed alarm at the position in France, but had expressed the greatest satisfaction when he had told them that there was no chance of our giving up the struggle. He did not remember having ever before heard a gathering of persons occupying high places in political life express themselves so emphatically."

Halifax now thought that he could not demur. He only referred to Reynaud's proposed appeal to Roosevelt.

Churchill "thought that an appeal to the United States at the present time would be altogether premature. If we made a bold stand against Germany, that would command their admiration and respect; but a grovelling appeal, if made now, would have the worst possible effect. He therefore did not favour making any approach on the subject at the present time."[29]

That was the end of it. He had worn down Halifax. Churchill left for Admiralty House, where he dined at half past eight and then drafted a late-night telegram to Reynaud. He told him that the War Cabinet had agreed: there was no reason to offer concessions to Mussolini now.[30]

That was the end of it. As Andrew Roberts properly wrote:

29. CAB 65/13.

30. Though, as a sop to Reynaud: " . . . without excluding the possibility of an approach to Signor Mussolini at some time, we cannot feel that this would be the right moment" (CAB 65/13. 235 Dipp. 28 May 1940). Yet "the effect on British morale, now resolute, would be dangerous. The situation could only be improved by showing that we still have stout hearts and confidence in ourselves. . . . If we both stand out we may yet save ourselves from the fate of Denmark or Poland" (Bell, *A Certain Eventuality,* 17: CAB 65/13, WM 145th conclusions).

"Churchill's instincts proved correct. Halifax had attempted to bring logic and reason to a problem long since devoid of either. . . . Halifax was right that there was nothing particularly patriotic in adopting a 'death or glory' attitude if the odds were on the former, any more than there was anything treacherous about attempting honourably to shorten a war Britain was clearly losing."[31] That is the best one can — and should — say about Halifax. But Churchill's best was — and proved to be — better than that.[32]

31. Roberts, *The Holy Fox*, 226.

32. "In October 1942, Sir Orme Sargent wrote Halifax about the way the events of 25 to 28 May ought to be portrayed in Sir Llewellyn Woodward's official history of the war. Halifax, who as early as February 1941 had shown disquiet about this, replied with a staggering lack of candour. He asserted, 'There was certainly never the idea in mind of HMG then or at any time of asking Mussolini to mediate terms between them and Germany,' and went on to imply that it had been solely neutrality from Italy and never mediation with Germany that had been the subject of the Bastianini conversation and subsequent Cabinet discussions. . . . Halifax insinuated that the most Britain had been willing to offer Italy was a seat on the board of the company which administered the Suez Canal. 'The holy Fox' could hear the hounds baying for his reputation, but he could lay only the faintest of false trails.

"He was not alone. Churchill wrote in *Their Finest Hour* how, 'Future generations may deem it noteworthy that the supreme question of whether we should fight on alone never found a place upon the War Cabinet agenda. . . . We were much too busy to waste time upon such academic, unreal issues.' In fact, future generations might find it just as noteworthy that there were five meetings [in reality, nine], some of which went on for as long as four hours, solely on that very subject" (ibid., 227–28).

CHAPTER SEVEN

Survival

A long-range view of the war. – The meaning of Dunkirk. –
"It is time to face up to facts." – Halifax redux. – An antiquated
Britain. – Churchill and Europe. – Fortissimo.

Historians are tempted to overstate the importance of their top-
ics, or their themes. This is why I am now compelled to argue my
case. Had Hitler won the Second World War we would be living in a
different world. That is not arguable. What is arguable is the crucial
importance of 24–28 May 1940, those five days in London. Was *that*
the hinge of fate? What if the Germans had won the air Battle of
Britain? What if Hitler had captured Moscow? What if he had won
at Stalingrad? What if D Day had failed? Any of these events could
have changed the course of the war. Yet my argument is that Hitler
was never closer to his ultimate victory than during those five days in
May 1940. This requires explanation — briefly.

The air Battle of Britain *was* very important, but it would not have
decided the entire outcome of the Second World War. A defeat of

the Royal Air Force would have made a German landing in England easier, but a successful invasion of England would still have been very difficult to manage. Hitler knew that: at first he was reluctant to begin the German air offensive, and only a few days after its start (on 14 August) he already knew that it would not be decisive. And what people did not know in 1940 was what we have learned since: that no great country can be conquered by air warfare alone. Also, Roosevelt's decision to range the United States more and more on the side of Britain was already made before the Battle of Britain.

Had Hitler captured Moscow or forced Stalin to seek some kind of a Russian capitulation, there is absolutely no evidence that the British (and the Americans) would not have fought on. The same applies to the event of a German conquest of Stalingrad.

Had D Day in June 1944 failed, perhaps Hitler and Stalin would have tried a deal; perhaps a second attempt to invade Western Europe would not have been possible in time; but there is not the slightest reason to believe that the Anglo-American alliance would have abandoned its determination to fight the Third Reich.

All this may seem overly optimistic and reliant on hindsight. There is, however, a very essential condition, or caveat, germane for the theme of this book. Had Hitler won at Moscow or at Stalingrad or in Normandy, he would not have won *his* war. But he may have been unbeatable. These two things are not the same. *His* aim was to dominate Europe and most of European Russia — and to make or force Britain and Russia and the United States to accept such a Germany victory of the Second World War. But by November 1941 at the latest, Hitler knew that this was no longer possible. Thereafter his strategy became "Friderician," reminiscent of that of Frederick the Great: to win sufficient victories to break up the unnatural coalition of his enemies — Anglo-Americans and Russians, capitalists and Communists, Churchill and Roosevelt and Stalin — and thus to compel one or the other to deal with him. This did not happen. Yet it could have happened. Had he triumphed in Russia, had he triumphed on the Normandy beaches, Churchill's and Roosevelt's position would have been very difficult, to say the least. That was how Hitler saw the war, and not unreasonably so. The defeat of the Soviet Union,[1] the defeat of the Anglo-Americans on the beaches, would not only have meant that the latter would have had to rethink their entire strategy; it would have led to possibly considerable opposition among the British and perhaps especially the American people to leaders who had declared that nothing but total victory over Germany, that is, nothing but its unconditional surrender, would do. In sum, Hitler could have forced his enemies to something like a draw.

All of this is speculation, but not speculation without substance. And I am compelled to sketch it in here in order to argue that the man in Hitler's way was Churchill. In May 1940 neither the United States nor Soviet Russia was at war with Germany. At that time there *were* reasons for a British government to at least ascertain whether a temporary compromise with Hitler was at all possible. Churchill thought and said no, that even the first cautious moves would mean stepping on a slippery slope; he was right, and not only morally speaking. Had Britain stopped fighting in May 1940, Hitler would have won *his* war. Thus he was never closer to victory than during those five days in May 1940. By the grace of God he did not know that. He thought that sooner or later (preferably sooner) Churchill would be forced to go. In this Hitler failed, because Churchill prevailed. Here I must repeat what I state on the first page of this book: Churchill and Britain could not have won the Second

---

1. Many people may have said, "At least Communism was defeated. And was that such a bad thing?"

World War; in the end America and Russia did. But in May 1940 Churchill was the one who did not *lose* it.[2]

That accounts for much, perhaps everything — including the saving grace (if that is what it was) of Dunkirk, and even of the Battle of Britain. We, the last surviving contemporaries of those May days, did not know that either. Many people do not know it now, which is the reason for my writing this book. I shall return to Dunkirk in a moment. Recall, however, that as late as 28 May few troops had been able to escape from Dunkirk; and, what is more important, that Churchill had declared that Britain would fight on, *whatever* might happen at Dunkirk. What then did happen there fortified his position; but it was his resolution that mattered.

On Wednesday, 29 May, Churchill's household routine returned to normal.[3] His new secretary, John Colville, wrote in his diary,

2. Here I must question the almost always unexceptionable and often brilliant Andrew Roberts, in the conclusion of his biography of Halifax: "The oft-repeated assertion that had Halifax become Prime Minister instead of Churchill 'we might have lost the war' is as hypothetical as it is hyperbolical. Churchill would still have been running the operational side, with Halifax providing the political leadership. History would have been denied morale-boosting speeches from No. 10, and Halifax might have been relegated to 'honorary' Prime Minister, but Britain would not have lost the war as a result" (Roberts, *The Holy Fox*, 308). I am not sure of this.

3. The record shows that he had the First Lord, A. V. Alexander, for lunch. During the afternoon an applicant for another household maid was being interviewed. He asked Chamberlain and Mrs. Chamberlain to dinner next night. During the day, too, came a handwritten note from the Treasury, an answer to Churchill's inquiry about his salary as prime minister, including his income tax reduction. It would be £1,737, 12 shillings and 7 pence (Churchill Diary, CA).

It was on this day that Churchill began to affix his later-famous slips of paper, with the phrase "Action This Day," on some of his orders.

"Winston's ceaseless industry is impressive." Among other things Churchill was encouraged by a strong letter from Cardinal Hinsley, the Roman Catholic primate of England: "The Cardinal is vigorous and tough, and I cannot see that it would do any harm, if he made it absolutely clear to his brethren over the water that, whatever happened, we are going to the end."[4] He was encouraged, too, by the developing news from Dunkirk, to which now, for the last time, we must turn.

♦ ♦ ♦

The turning point at Dunkirk was that day, Wednesday, the twenty-ninth of May. That morning Gort still thought that further evacuation might become impossible, yet as the day went on the prospects brightened. That day and night more than 47,000 men were lifted off from the Dunkirk mole and from the beaches, nearly three times as many as the day before. (On 30 May there would be 53,800, on 31 May 68,000, on 1 June 64,400; thereafter the numbers would diminish to 26,000 for each of the remaining three days of evacuation. The number of French troops carried off by British vessels did not significantly increase until 31 May, and then on Churchill's direct orders. By the end of day 4 June, the grand totals were 338,226, including more than 125,000 French.) The bombing raids of the Luftwaffe were severe on the twenty-ninth; moreover, the Germans were moving close enough to Dunkirk for their field artillery to begin shelling the town, not only from the south but also from the west. There were more than a few ugly scenes of low morale, including violent misunderstandings between the British and the French, but generally enough discipline and organization prevailed, which was not easy amid conditions of frequent retreating and the unprecedented and often chaotic situation on the beaches. Especially along the perimeter the French fought as well as the

4. PREM 4/22/3.

British.[5] At the end of the day Churchill, overoptimistically, sent a message to Spears to give to Reynaud: nearly 50,000 were evacuated and "hope another 30,000 tonight. Front may be beaten in at any time or place, beaches and shipping rendered unusable by air attacks, and also artillery fire from the South-West. No one can tell how long present good flow will last, or how much we can save for future. We wish French troops to share in evacuation to fullest possible extent."

"Front may be beaten in . . ." Churchill was becoming aware that the Germans were cautious, that they were not making a direct thrust into Dunkirk proper. On 31 May General Fedor von Bock wrote in his diary, "When we finally arrive in Dunkirk [the English] will be gone!" He was inclined to blame Rundstedt; he thought that, wishing to spare his armor, Rundstedt had influenced Hitler. Perhaps their influences were reciprocal. There is a minute by Churchill on 2 June to the chiefs of staff suggesting that he recognized some of this: the returning British troops were men "whose mettle [the Germans] had already tested, and from whom they have recoiled, not daring seriously to molest their departure."[6] Ironside wrote in his diary on the same day: "I still cannot understand how it is that the Bosches [sic] have allowed us to get the B.E.F. off in this way. It is almost fantastic that we have been able to do it in the face of all the bombing and gunning."[7]

5. General Ismay at the War Cabinet that morning: "The French were disinclined to retire, but Lord Gort was urging them to come back as the British could not wait for them" (CAB 65/13, WM 146).

6. Churchill to Ismay, CA 20.13. In a later letter to the prime ministers of the Dominions about the air fighting over Dunkirk, Churchill wrote that Dunkirk was a sort of no-man's-land.

7. "It brings me to the fact that the Bosches may equally well be able to

Hitler was a secretive man. We shall never know what were the purposes (let alone the motives) of his halt order, on 24 May, to allow the siege of Dunkirk to depend first on Goering's air force. We saw that he gave several explanations — or, rather, justifications — to his own circle later, the last time before the end of the war, in 1945, when he said that he had given Churchill "a sporting chance" which the latter failed to appreciate. That was surely a rationalization.[8] Hitler could be outspoken; but he was not honest. On 31 May he wrote to Mussolini, who had informed him that Italy would enter the war on 5 June; he did not say a word about how he hoped to influence the British. To the contrary. He said that the British were being destroyed in Flanders: "Only a very small percentage of defeated men . . . reach the English coast." He also asked Mussolini to postpone Italy's entry into the war by a few more days.[9] He wanted to achieve his victory alone.

Churchill was less secretive, more honest. "Having survived a most serious challenge to his leadership," I wrote in *The Duel*, "and then having avoided a British catastrophe at Dunkirk, his resolution (perhaps more than his confidence) was as strong, if not stronger, than before" — while Hitler's "confidence was stronger than his

———————————

land men in England despite the bombing. Had the Germans had any Navy they might have upset our embarkation. What have their submarines been doing?" (*The Ironside Diaries*).

8. His first rationalization occurred on 2 June, recorded by General Halder's representative at Hitler's headquarters: there was "a slight difference between Italy and Germany. Italy's main enemy had become England. Germany's main enemy was France," and the British would soon be ready for a "reasonable conclusion of peace" (Halder's War Diary, cited in Lukacs, *The Duel*, 105).

9. *Documenti diplomatici italiani, 1939–1943,* series 9, vol. 4, 520.

resolution. He was still speculating about what the English might do." Churchill telegraphed to Keyes late on 28 May, after the Belgian king's decision to surrender to Hitler: "What can we do for him? . . . Our only hope is victory and England will never quit the war whatever happens *till Hitler is beat or we cease to be a state.*"[10] The italics are mine. Churchill had survived Halifax's challenge. But his real opponent was not Halifax but Hitler. His hands were, perhaps temporarily, free. Yet one's hands may be free, but one's arm might not be strong enough. Churchill knew that very well. His mind was now preoccupied with the question, Would the Germans attempt to invade England even before their conquest of France? He thought no; in that he was right. But he was wrong in thinking — or, rather, hoping — that the French might still hold the Germans, somewhere in France, no matter where. That would not happen. Still he was prepared for the worst. One example of that appears in his detailed minute to General Ismay on this very busy day of 29 May, where he is impetuous about the need for a reorganization of the army in England and sets forth a detailed and radical proposal summed up in four short paragraphs.[11]

Within the War Cabinet not much of grave importance happened on this day. There was a long discussion about instructions to Gort at Dunkirk and also about the evacuation of Narvik in northern Norway. Halifax spoke only once: "He was not altogether happy over the very definite instructions that had been given [to Gort]. He agreed that the grim struggle must continue, but he would like a

10. In his great speech on 4 June, Churchill was not as fair to Leopold III as he had been on 28 May. (The London correspondent of the *Manchester Guardian,* 30 May: "There has been a generous impulse, surprisingly general, to leave King Leopold to his conscience and to history.")

11. PREM 3/22/13.

message sent to Lord Gort expressing the implicit trust that the Government placed in him and on any action that he would see fit to take in the last resort. It would not be dishonourable to relinquish the struggle in order to save a handful of men from massacre." Churchill said "that in a desperate situation any brave man was entitled, in the absence of precise orders to the contrary, to use his own discretion, and that therefore he would not modify the instructions to Lord Gort. Our object was to ensure the evacuation of every possible man, and then the infliction of the maximum possible damage to the enemy. A day gained might well meant a further 40,000 men taken off. A Commander, in circumstances as desperate and distressing as those in which Lord Gort now found himself, should not be offered the difficult choices between resistance and capitulation."[12] That was the last flicker of open conflict between Churchill and Halifax in the War Cabinet.

Cadogan was present and wrote a bleak account in his diary: "News unpleasant. We have got off 40,000 men and taking them, at present, at the rate of 2,000 an hour. But the end will be awful. A horrible discussion of what instructions to send to Gort. W.S.C. rather theatrically bulldoggish. Opposed by [Chamberlain and Halifax] and yielded to a reasonable extent. Fear relations will become rather strained. That is Winston's fault . . . theatricality . . . " Yet two days later: "By noon we have taken off 164,000 men — a miracle!" The next day: "Cabinet 11:30, evacuation marvellous."[13]

There is no question that the ultimate result of Dunkirk was a great boon to Churchill's prestige. Had the Germans captured the bulk of the British army there, forcing it to surrender, the blaze of such a great Hitlerian triumph would have cast a large dark shadow

12. CAB 65/13, WM 146.
13. Cadogan, *Diaries,* 292, 293.

on the island people, involving hundreds of thousands of prisoners of their own, and perhaps on Churchill's position and prospects, too. Yet, as we have seen, he had declared that he and Britain would fight on, no matter what happened at Dunkirk; and he seems to have had the majority of the British people behind him. Something of the same happened when France finally fell; it did not really affect his leadership and his prestige. He of course knew that Dunkirk was not a victory. As he said as early as 4 June, "Wars are not won by evacuations." Around that time he first met the later-famous General Bernard Law Montgomery, who was angry at how many people saw Dunkirk as a victory: "He criticized the shoulder ribbons issued to the troops, marked 'Dunkirk.' They were not 'heroes.' 'If it was not understood' that the army suffered a defeat at Dunkirk, then 'our island home was now in grave danger.'"[14] Churchill saw things in much the same way. He understood the unpreparedness of the army, facing a possible invasion. He was worried, too, about British morale. Since that time many people (and a few then, too) have seen Dunkirk as a necessary myth. Others have seen it as something like the Battle of the Marne in 1914. The truth may be somewhere in between.

In any event, on 29 May 1940 the unfolding of the eventual result of Dunkirk was only at its beginning. Neither the War Cabinet nor the British people knew that. The reactions of the latter ran, as so often, behind the course of events. For the purposes of this book, which is not a military history, their reconstruction is as essential as a summation of what was happening at Dunkirk; probably more so.

◆ ◆ ◆

We have seen that until the late afternoon of 29 May Churchill himself was not confident about the survival of most of the army

14. Lukacs, *The Duel*, 144.

closed in at Dunkirk. Among the British people, opinion and the press that day showed a grim pessimism; it took two or three days for them to catch up with the development of events, to recognize the first brightening news from Dunkirk. The newspapers of 29 May (keep in mind that most of their texts had been composed the night before) reflected this. The lead article of the 29 May *News Chronicle* was typical: "It is time to face up to the facts, to admit the worst. With the surrender of the Belgian Army the B.E.F. seems to be cut off. Escape by the sea is the slenderest of hopes. A break through the south is a possibility equally remote."[15] The front page of the *Daily Mail* carried the headline "How the B.E.F. Was Trapped." The accompanying article, written by the paper's correspondent with the BEF, began: "The British Expeditionary Force today is almost surrounded. That is the very grave position caused by the surrender of the Belgian Army." Many of the papers still gave considerable space to the Belgian news of the day before. The *Daily Express:* "We must keep all our anger for our one enemy, Hitler."[16] The leading article in the *Daily Telegraph:* "Nothing is gained by blinking facts or mincing words. The British Expeditionary Force and the French divisions with it are beset on three sides and from the air. All are in danger of being cut off from Dunkirk." On the same page were two articles praising the French: "The effect of the disastrous break of the line [that is, the Belgian capitulation] is a hardening of resolution"; France "had stood up heroically to the hard knock of the Belgian

15. "Stock Exchange Not Dismayed."

16. The widely known columnist William Hickey: "To the English people, Leopold's surrender was as incredible as it was disquieting"; "in a teashop I heard a woman say, plaintively: 'But he was such a nice-looking boy.' In an expensive grill-room I heard a man say: 'I'm terribly shocked about it. He was at Eton.' "

surrender. . . . The Paris public is showing a stoicism of a kind often described as Anglo-Saxon." (Perhaps this was whistling in the dark. However, it is true that morale in Paris did not crack until about 10 June.) The *Yorkshire Post*, like other newspapers in the counties, were emphatic in praising national unity and the new government.

The Mass-Observation analysis of *Morale* gave this summary: "Roughly speaking, people are at present calm but exceedingly anxious. . . . For whereas before people were more confident in victory, without a glimmering of what the struggle for victory might mean, now they realise to a considerable extent what they are up against. They do not realise fully, especially those, the majority, who left school when they were fourteen and have never crossed the channel or spoken to a German. But at least the period of utter wishful thinking is over."[17]

At night on 29 May Harold Nicolson wrote his diary, "We are creating a Corunna Line along the beaches around Dunkirk and hope to evacuate a few of our troops." (This shows that Nicolson, now in a high position in the Ministry of Information, did not quite comprehend the situation: what had happened at Corunna in 1809 bore little similarity to Dunkirk in 1940, and when Nicolson wrote these lines many more than a few troops had been lifted off to England.)[18] Two days later Nicolson wrote to his wife: "My darling

17. "London consistently shows more anxiety . . . than the provinces" (FR 159).

18. "I find a passionate letter from the French Ambassador saying that our Press is putting all the blame on the French Army. [This was not so.] . . . We hope to improve the situation. . . . The work is urgent and cumulative as during the Paris Peace Conference. But then we were happy in those days and not in a state of fear" (*The Diaries and Letters of Harold Nicolson*, 91). In his unpublished diary entries, Nicolson records meeting the American cor-

how *infectious* courage is. I am rendered far stronger in heart and confidence by such bravery." The same day, in Oxford, C. S. Lewis wrote to Owen Barfield: "And oddly enough, I notice that since things got really bad, everyone I meet is less dismayed. . . . Even at this present moment I don't feel nearly so bad as I should have done if anyone had prophesied to me eighteen months ago."[19]

Recalling those days, Margery Allingham later wrote to her American friends: "You are warm people; we are cold people who have been warm and still have warmth in places. Our heart is old and hard and true still, in spite of surface rot." About 29–30 May she mused: "Let me see. Somebody complained about the quality of the knitting of the comforts. Somebody else thought the pig club must be a twist.

---

respondent Vincent Sheean that night: "an absolute worshipper of Winston Churchill. He is going to devote all the influence he has to bringing America to our assistance. He says our greatest danger is that the isolationists are now concentrating upon the argument that it is too late for them to help England."

19. Cited in Lukacs, *The Last European War,* 417. This is not the gloomy fatalism that we get from the recollections of Leonard (and of Virginia) Woolf: "We also crammed as much social life as possible into our four days, having many of our friends for dinner. For instance, in the two London visits of May 21–24 and June 4–7 we saw T. S. Eliot, Koteliansky, William Plomer, Sybil Colefax, Morgan Forster, Raymond Mortimer, Stephen Spender, Kingsley Martin, Rose Macaulay, and Willie Robson.

"There was in those days an ominous and threatening unreality, a feeling that one was living in a bad dream, and that one was on the point of waking up from this horrible unreality into a still more horrible reality. . . . There was a curious atmosphere of quiet fatalism, of waiting for the inevitable and the aura of it still lingers in the account of our days in London which Virginia gives in her diary" (Leonard Woolf, *The Journey Not the Arrival Matters,* 53–54).

Somebody refused to take in evacuees. Somebody said we were cowards to retreat to Dunkirk and ought to have gone on and beaten up everybody. Somebody said they would rather let their fruit rot than let the Women's Institute lay hands on it. And so on. Now I come to look at it, nobody *did* anything un-cooperative. It was all talk and we are fighting to say what we like. Unimportant remarks all of them and the devil's own job to remember after a month or two, as I can testify."[20]

Vera Brittain later recalled the last days of May in London: "Martin and I walk in Regent's Park amid shaded mauve pansies and pale pink lupins. 'It's just like a Sunday,' I remark to him, for the Park is so deserted that it suggests a hot summer holiday when everyone who possesses something on wheels has gone into the country. Since most of the iron railings have now been removed from London's parks and squares for conversion into armaments, Regent's Park resembled a vast green field, very fresh and vivid. A few elderly people are sitting in chairs, a few young ones sailing in boats with striped sails. Again . . . comes the strange illusion of peace, due largely to the beauty of the summer and its scents and sounds. We feel as though we are watching the funeral of European civilisations elegantly conducted. Just so the Roman Empire must have appeared before the barbarians marched in."[21]

♦ ♦ ♦

Hitler did have some snippets of intelligence about what was or what was not going on in London in May 1940. He was hoping and planning, and then hoping, and, after July, hoping against hope, that there would be a break in London and that the British would get rid of Churchill. This was the essential matter: for never, throughout

20. Allingham, *The Oaken Heart*, 255.
21. Brittain, *England's Hour*, 41.

the entire war, were Hitler's hopes more warranted then during those five days — that is, before the ending of Dunkirk, before the surrender of France, and before the air offensive against Britain. But there was a time lag involving his intelligence and information. It was only in early June that he began to request and collect and read every kind of intelligence information concerning London. (Contrary to accepted views, he read much, and quickly.) Churchill was aware of this; on occasion (especially in July) he allowed the feeding of odd kinds of ambiguous information to German agents abroad, with the purpose of making Hitler hesitate and delay his invasion preparations. To this we may add that the British achievement of breaking into German military codes ("Enigma" and, later, "Ultra") was but fragmentary and fledgling in the summer of 1940. But all of that belongs to the later months of their duel, not to May.

For Churchill, Dunkirk, while not a victory, was of course a relief. But that relief was short-lived, soon to be overcast by the vast meaning of the fall of France. Immediately after Dunkirk Churchill made one of his greatest speeches, on 4 June. Immediately after the collapse of the French government he made another famous one, on 18 June. Yet the immediate effect of these speeches on the British people was limited. Their effect was cumulative (or, to use Cardinal Newman's favorite adjective, illative).

On 28 May a paper from the Foreign Office suggested that " 'most secret plans' should be considered both for the evacuation of the Royal Family and the government 'to some part of the Overseas Empire, whence the war could continue to be waged if circumstances prevented their continuation from the United Kingdom,' and for the removal *now* from Britain 'to another part of the Empire' of the Crown Jewels, the Coronation Chair, gold bullion, securities and precious stones." On 1 June Churchill rejected this in a memorandum: "I believe we shall make them rue the day they try to invade our island. No such discussion can be permitted."[22] Yet General Pownall recollected that "sometime in early June" Winston said, in this connection, "I *wonder* if we can hold them": "An insight into his real thoughts. Great morale-raising speeches, necessary as they are, do not necessarily, or even often, reflect the inward opinions of those who make them."[23]

Except for a few unimportant occasions, Edward Halifax no longer chose to oppose Churchill in the War Cabinet. (Indeed, on 13 June, on one occasion he adopted Churchill's own phrase "the slippery slope": if the French were to ask for an armistice "they would embark on a slippery slope, which would lead to a loss of their fleet, and eventually of their liberty."[24] Yet in his diaries (written, as we know, for circulation within his family) he was on occasion still very critical of Churchill.[25] Then there was the incident on

---

22. Gilbert, *Companion Volume*, 187 n. 1.

23. Pownall, *Chief of Staff* 2:359. Note, however, Churchill's habit of openly speculating and frankly discussing the most important matters within his circle. Sir Edward Bridges: "In this sort of discussion he would keep nothing back. He would express the most outspoken views . . . or about the various ways in which the situation might be expected to develop" (*Action This Day,* 22–23).

24. Lukacs, *The Duel,* 103.

25. 30 May, after a cabinet: "Winston was in a combative and discursive mood. I have never seen so disorderly a mind. I am coming to the conclusion that his process of thought is one that had to operate through speech. As this is exactly the reverse of my own, it is irritating." 19 June: "It is the most extraordinary brain, Winston's, to watch functioning that I have ever seen, a most curious mixture of a child's emotion and a man's reason." 24 June: "Winston's garrulousness . . . " (Halifax Papers, A.7.8.4). These diaries are weeded. His correspondence with his wife, who disliked Churchill, is still kept in a sealed hamper in the Muniment Room, Garrowby. On

17 June — the darkest day, the morning after Pétain had replaced Reynaud in France, when the French capitulation became a certainty. "Rab" Butler, Halifax's undersecretary, met the Swedish minister to London, Björn Prytz, in St. James's Park. He asked Prytz to come up to his office. There he told Prytz that "no opportunity would be neglected for concluding a compromise peace if the chance offered of reasonable conditions. . . . the so-called diehards [suggesting Churchill] would not be allowed to stand in the way of negotiations." Prytz was still in Butler's office when Butler went over to see Halifax. When he came back to the room, Butler told Prytz that Halifax had a message for him: "Common sense and not bravado would dictate the British government's policy" — even though Prytz should not interpret that to mean peace at any price. In his urgent telegram to Stockholm, Prytz added that his conversation with other prominent Englishmen (mostly certain members of Parliament) suggested that Halifax might replace Churchill at the head of the government in about ten days. The Italian minister to Stockholm, learning of this in a few hours, exaggerated the importance of this news, reporting (wrongly) that the British minister to Stockholm had approached the Swedish government with an inquiry about peace proposals. This was not so. A day later Prytz himself corrected the meaning of his first telegram. These details are known by diplomatic historians of the period.[26] To this we may add a letter from Churchill to Halifax, now available in the Churchill Archives, dated 25 June: "My dear Edward. It is quite clear to me from these telegrams and others that Butler held odd language to the Swedish

---

5 July Halifax said to Victor Cazalet that Churchill was getting to be arrogant and impatient: "It's almost impossible to get five minutes of conversation with him" (Gilbert, *Companion Volume*, 483–84).

26. Lukacs, *The Duel*, 132–33, also 150–51.

Minister and certainly the Swede derived a strong impression of defeatism. In these circumstances would it not be well for you to find out from Butler what actually he did say. [In the Secret Session of the House of Commons I gave] assurances that the present Government and all its members were resolved to fight on to the death, and I did so, taking personal responsibility for the resolve of all."[27] Halifax answered three days later, defending Butler. There the case rested. When Hitler made his grand peace offer to England in his speech of 19 July, Churchill chose not to answer, asking Halifax to do so instead, which the foreign secretary calmly and coolly did.

In December 1940 Churchill asked Halifax to become ambassador to the United States, replacing him at the Foreign Office with Anthony Eden (who was not the best choice, Churchillian though he was). Lady Halifax was abashed. Yet Halifax turned out to be an excellent ambassador. (That was also largely true of other anti-Churchillians, such as Samuel Hoare, whom Churchill virtually exiled from London in May, appointing him ambassador to Spain. The patriotism of these Englishmen — unlike that of many ambassadors of many other countries at critical posts — unquestionably prevailed over their political or ideological inclinations.)

It is interesting to note that what his biographer Andrew Roberts has called Halifax's Whiggism — or his inclination to think in pragmatic political terms — predominated throughout, surpassing his personal or ideological or even religious beliefs. In July 1944 Hugh Dalton noted in his diary a conversation with Halifax: "He was quite sure that we must never let ourselves get into the state of mind of asking whether it was better to co-operate with the Americans or with the Russians. We must do our utmost with both and, in particular, must always treat the Russians with the greatest consider-

27. CA, 20/2.

ation, and never let them think that we were having secrets with the Americans from which they were excluded."[28] Halifax was still ambassador to Washington in March 1946, when Churchill made his famous Iron Curtain speech in Fulton, Missouri. Halifax was down with influenza and dictated a message to his wife for Churchill, the gist of which was that Churchill should not have been so tough about Soviet Russia, that Stalin "completely misunderstood what you said at Fulton," and that because of their wartime relationship Churchill should think of going to Moscow to talk to Stalin.[29] (So much from a pillar of the Church of England. Someone once asked Churchill about his relationship to the church. Was he a pillar of the church—perhaps like Halifax? No, said Churchill: but he was a flying buttress.)

◆ ◆ ◆

Returning to June 1940, let us now make a fast run through the great events of the summer, during which Churchill rose to be the savior of England.[30] On 4 June Dunkirk fell to the Germans. Six days later Mussolini declared war. Another week later France

28. *The Second World War Diaries of Hugh Dalton,* 767. Contrast this with Churchill in October 1943, as recorded by Pownall, *Chief of Staff* 2:109–10: Churchill "thoroughly dislikes the Russians and their ways and is under no illusions about them. They are doing what they are doing (and very well too) to save their own skins. Their future policy will be entirely to suit themselves and nobody else will count. All the more necessary, of course, to keep along with the U.S."

29. Halifax Papers, A.7.7.18. Churchill then telephoned (on 14 March) to Lady Halifax; he was grateful for the suggestion but couldn't do it: "It would be 'the whipped cur coming to heel,' and like going to see Hitler just before the war."

30. This phrase, or designation, appears in one of the biographical footnotes in A. J. P. Taylor, *English History.*

capitulated to Hitler. The latter still hoped to hear promising news from England. There was none. The British people were now fortified by Churchill's leadership and by his words.[31] On 16 July Hitler issued his somewhat cautiously phrased directive to prepare for the invasion of England. Three days later he made his long-prepared victory speech, in which he made a last proposal for peace to England while attacking Churchill in violent terms. There was no response from London. On 31 July Hitler summoned his generals, telling them to prepare for a war against Soviet Russia. There was more method than madness in that decision. He said that England had only two hopes, America and Russia. Against America he could do nothing. But if Russia were eliminated, England's last hope for a possible ally in Europe would vanish, and the Americans would have their hands full with Japan.

On that very day, 31 July, Franklin Roosevelt began to move. Before the end of July he was not sure that Britain would hold out; if not, the New World would receive the British fleet.[32] Now he pre-

31. The statistics from a public opinion survey, "Approve or Disapprove of the Prime Minister," were as follows: Chamberlain, November 1939, 68 percent; January 1940, 56 percent; 9–10 May 1940, 32 percent. For Churchill: July 1940, 88 percent; disapprove, 7 percent; don't know, 5 percent.

32. See the developing exchange of communications between him and Churchill through that summer in *Churchill and Roosevelt: The Complete Correspondence.* This important and unique collection (they exchanged more than two thousand letters during the war, in addition to their often unrecorded telephone conversations) is marred by some of the egregious comments ("Headnotes") by the editor, Warren F. Kimball. For example, about their exchange on the crucial days of 14–15 June, Kimball writes that Churchill, "distraught, . . . found it necessary to warn Roosevelt that Great Britain could not be expected to fight on alone without any real hope of American military intervention. His threat that a pro-German government

pared to skirt Congress and offer fifty old destroyers to Britain, a drastic departure from American neutrality. This was announced on 2/3 September, exactly one year after Britain had gone to war with Germany. Meanwhile, the Battle of Britain went on in the air. The Germans did not defeat the British fighter force. On 7 September Hitler ordered the switching of the air offensive to the bombing of London. On 16 September he postponed the invasion project. Four days later he corralled the eager Japanese into an alliance expressly directed against the United States. On the last day of the year President Roosevelt announced the Lend-Lease Act in support of Britain, stating that the United States was henceforth the arsenal of democracy.

London was now the capital of freedom, the fountain of hope for millions of Europeans who listened night after night to the broadcasts of the British Broadcasting Corporation. That inspiring condition would last throughout the war. But long before the end of the war it began to appear that the price of victory over Hitler would be a different England and a different civilization — and not only because Britain had no chance of winning the war alone. The germs of these developments were already latent in the first days of June.

On Sunday, 9 June, Charles de Gaulle flew to London for the first time. "The English capital had a look of tranquillity, almost indifference. The streets and parks full of people peacefully out for a walk, the long queues at the entrances to the cinemas, the many cars, the impressive porters outside the clubs and hotels, belonged to another

---

might replace his Ministry was the first and one of the very few times that Churchill ever strayed from his usual strategy of emphasizing Britain's willingness to fight to the bitter end." It was not said for the first time; it was not a threat but a warning of something that had to be kept in mind; and it did not represent Churchill "straying."

world than the one at war." His conclusion was not optimistic: "The mass of the population had no idea of the gravity of events in France. . . . It was plain, in any case, that to English minds the Channel was still wide."[33] Elegant London may have disappointed de Gaulle, yet (yes, the Channel was still wide) the reactions (and the memories) of many Englishmen and Englishwomen were not disappointing. Mrs. Robert Henrey remembered those early days in June: "London is always a joy to walk back into, . . . its colouring so vivid that it blinded me. How elegant the women in Fortnum and Mason! How numerous the expensive cars in Piccadilly."[34] Mrs. Henrey took heart from this. So did many others; foreigners and Anglophiles, whether in England or not: they saw the elegance and the untroubled calm as a living symbol of a Western high bourgeois civilization, representing the very antithesis of the heavy brutality incarnated by Hitler and his Germans.

Then France fell. As early as March 1938 General Pownall cited the words of Queen Elizabeth in the sixteenth century: "Whensoever the last day of the Kingdom of France cometh it will undoubtedly be the event of the destruction of England."[35] On 16 June 1940 Pownall wrote in his diary: "In London it can be hardly said that people are cheerful, there's little enough to be cheerful about. But they are calm and resigned to the probability that when Hitler was finished with France he will turn on England. They don't realise of course what it means to be 'turned on' by the power of Germany." Next day he wrote: "As nations we have got fat and lazy. We possessed great Empires, earned for us by the sweat and blood of our ancestors, that we would not take sufficient care to defend. Hitler

33. Charles de Gaulle, *War Memoirs*, 62–63.
34. Henrey, *London Under Fire*, 15.
35. From Raleigh, *English Voyages of the Sixteenth Century*, 70.

has at least inspired the spirit of self-sacrifice in his nation — with us there is no such spirit of service. . . . Democracies are inefficient, in war and in preparation for war, compared to autocracies; add to this the sapping of morale which democracy brings with its pandering to the public and its competition for votes."[36] He thought that the lines from *Henry VI*, part 1, act 1, scene 1, are "strangely apt":

GLOUCESTER. Is Paris lost? Is Rouen yielded up? . . .
EXETER. How were they lost? What treachery was used?
MESSENGER. No treachery, but want of men and money;
  Among the soldiers, this is muttered —
  That here you maintain several factions,
  And whilst a field should be despatched and fought,
  You are disputing of your generals:
  One would have lingering wars, with little cost:
  Another would fly swift, but wanteth wings:
  A third man thinks, without expense at all,
  By guileful fair words peace may be obtained.
  Awake, awake, English nobility!

In more than one way, these Shakespearean lines were "strangely apt." But Pownall was too pessimistic about the effects of the fall of France and perhaps about democracy too. A very different man from Pownall was George Orwell. He, too, was not inspired by what Mrs. Henrey saw. Later that year Orwell wrote that "the lady in the Rolls-Royce car is more damaging to morale than a fleet of Goering's bombing-planes." He may have been wrong.[37] Yet in 1940 Orwell's

36. Pownall, *Chief of Staff*, 368–69.
37. Surely not as wrong as the German refugee writer Franz Borkenau, whom Orwell quoted in his wartime diary: "Franz Borkenau says England is now definitely in the first stage of revolution" (341).

patriotism (and his traditionalism) rose to tower high above his democratic class-consciousness. In 1944, in "The English Class System," he wrote, "It is significant that in the moment of disaster the man best able to unite the nation was Churchill, a Conservative of aristocratic origins." (It is no less significant that in 1947 Orwell gave the name Winston Smith to his hero in *1984,* that Winston was born and so christened in 1945, and that in his first act of revolt against darkness and oppression, Winston Smith raises his glass and toasts the Past.)

"Conservative" and "aristocratic": we must, for the last time, consider these adjectives. Beaverbrook—another man very different from both Pownall and Orwell—recalled in a speech in 1964: "We were so ill-prepared. Our peril was beyond comprehension. Churchill, after taking office, said to me: 'We will come through in triumph but we may lose our tail feathers.' "[38] More than tail feathers— but perhaps that is not the point. The "reactionary" Churchill (and that was how such different men as Halifax and Hitler saw him) was both more and less conservative than were many men of his party. He was both more and less aristocratic than were some of his British critics, many of whom may have thought that without tail feathers there can be no respectability. Chips Channon, who fervently supported Chamberlain and who distrusted and disliked Churchill, wrote in his diary on the night of 28 May, when Churchill had had his way: "I think there is a definite plot afoot to oust Halifax, and all the gentlemen of England, from the Government and even from the House of Commons."[39] All the gentlemen of England . . . We have seen that there were not a few people, perhaps especially among the Conservative members in the House, who thought that Churchill

38. Cited in Smith, *The English Reader,* 120.
39. Cited in Lukacs, *The Duel,* 100.

was not quite a gentleman. They sat on their hands in May, not much inclined to applaud Churchill. Even in June the silence of many of the Tories was "sinister." It was not until July that the majority of the Conservative members of Parliament thought it best to express their loyalty to Churchill.[40] They had been elected in 1935, most of them Chamberlainites in 1937 and after, convinced that they represented respectable opinion in England. Respectability was the key. (Someone who knew them both once said to me: "I respected Halifax more than I liked him," but "I respected Churchill less than I liked him.")

The deep-seated conservatism of the British people — as distinct from the political and social conservatism of the Conservatives — was a great asset in 1940. The great majority did not know — more precisely, they were hardly able to conceive — that Britain might lose the war. Within their patriotism (it was old-fashioned patriotism, rather than modern nationalism) there was of course an element of their pride as well as their sense of history. We can see some of this in a moving diary entry written by a sensitive middle-class woman on 5 June: "This morning I lingered over my breakfast, reading and re-reading the accounts of the Dunkirk evacuation. I felt as if deep inside me there was a harp that vibrated and sang — like the feeling on a hillside of gorse in the hot bright sun, or seeing suddenly, as you walked through a park, a big bed of clear, thin red poppies in all their brave splendour. I forgot I was a middle-aged woman who

40. Roberts, in *Eminent Churchillians,* about the Tories versus Churchill: "The tale has therefore to be pieced together from scraps among hundreds of public and private sources. When it is, the picture which emerges is radically different from the accepted Tory version" (138). They hate "the wild man" (160). Even after July 1940, and unlike what many historians had written: "the Tory Party was still suspicious of him" (183).

often got up tired and also had backache. . . . It was a very hot morning and work was slowed a little, but somehow I felt everything to be worthwhile, and I felt glad I was of the same race as the rescuers and rescued."[41]

The British people did not know how antiquated was the condition of their country when compared to that of Germany in 1940. This was so not only with regard to the armaments of the two nations or their military tactics; it was also so with regard to the structure of their societies. The traditions of British democracy and the British system of classes were old; compared to them the institutions and also the developing social structure of Hitler's Germany, of his populist folk-state, were more modern.[42] The conditions of

---

41. *Nella's Last War,* 62.

42. One startling and shocking evidence of this was the general failure of the evacuation of children from London at the start of the war (the government project in view of possible air raids). More than a million working-class children were sent to middle-class homes in the country, often with their mothers. "The scheme has now [this was written in the late spring of 1940] frittered away, and the sociologist's job is to record what happened. . . . As it is, thousands of hosts in reception areas are disgruntled and would be unwilling to experiment with further visitors, and thousands of mothers have gone back to the danger zones with their minds made up never to return" (*War Begins at Home,* 296). One M-O observer: "The gulf between middle-class hosts and workers' child-evacuees is somewhat unbridgeable; the utter destitution of some children [many of them lice-ridden and verminous] evokes horror among the middle classes. In one case a woman was driven mad by the vile filth and disease of two children. It is doubtful if she will recover" (312). Another: "The main drawback of the evacuation scheme was that it underestimated the difference which exists between various sections of the population" (306). Nothing like this in the Third Reich.

British industry and finance, British habits and fashions and customs of communication, British modes of behavior and thought, were still old-fashioned, in the literal sense of that adjective. It is not sufficient to attribute these conditions to the national weariness or to the languid decadence that followed the First World War. There were many late-Victorian or Edwardian habits, physical and mental, extant in 1940. So were many of the sounds and smells and sights: organ music in the cinemas, coal smoke, flowered frocks on the greenswards, the tastes of strong tea and weak cocoa, Anglican clergymen in gaiters, club silence and pub talk. From examining some of the private letters of the times — not only their contents but their very paper and often their handwriting — one gets the sense of a place and an age that is *old*. The shock of May–June 1940, together with Churchill's leadership quality, then produced a wonderful fillip of national unity and hard work and discipline. But 1940 was still, the end of an entire age — or, rather, the beginning of its end.

◆ ◆ ◆

Churchill saw Hitler and his Reich as incarnating something evil and dangerous, some of the brutal sources of which may have been very old but some of which were also alarmingly new. And his vision was such that he turned out to be the savior not only of England but of much else besides — essentially, of all Europe. He was very much aware of this. On 28 May he spoke "of the world cause to which we have vowed ourselves." On 14 July he declared that Britain was fighting "*by* ourselves alone, but not *for* ourselves alone." London "was this strong City of Refuge which enshrines the title-deeds of human progress and is of deep consequence to Christian civilisation." In 1941, in a broadcast to the United States: "In these British Islands that look so small upon the map we stand, the faithful guardians of the right and dearest hopes of a dozen States and nations now gripped and tormented in a base and cruel servitude." That concern with Europe had been one of the main differences between the vision of Churchill and that of Halifax and indeed of most Conservatives.[43] Memories of his ancestor Marlborough and the Edwardian elements in his character may have moved him. But there was more to it than that. Churchill did not for a moment believe that Britain and the Empire could continue to exist across from a Europe entirely dominated by Germany. If the price of survival of British independence and British democracy was the eventual transference of much of the imperial burden to the Americans, so be it; and if the price of winning the war was the tacit acceptance of Russian overlordship over much of Eastern Europe, that was unavoidable, too: for half of Europe (including of course all of Western Europe) was better than none.[44]

So much for his vision — and for his strategy. That much we can see in retrospect. But it is important to recognize that this was the essence of his vision and of his strategy even in May and June 1940,

43. Andrew Roberts: Halifax "made the disastrous error of trying to translate his Indian experiences of dealing with Congress into policy dealing with the problems of Europe" (*The Holy Fox,* 41). Kenneth Rose: "What tarnishes the memory of the so-called appeasers is not that they were deterred from robustness by the strategic and economic realities of a defence policy; it is the sycophancy with which they witnessed the creeping enslavement of Europe" (*King George V,* 84).

44. But Churchill also knew that the limits of the Russian occupation of Eastern Europe ought to be defined and kept as far from the center as possible (in this the Americans did not support him) and that, as he said to de Gaulle in November 1944, this Russian rule would not last ("After the meal comes the digestion period"). To Colville, on New Year's Day in 1953, he predicted that by the 1980s Communism would disappear from Eastern Europe.

when a British-inspired and British-managed liberation of Europe was not in the cards. To the contrary: that was the moment when not only his domestic opponents but many of the defeated peoples of Western Europe were inclined to accept the collapse of parliamentary democracy and seek some kind of accommodation with the triumphant Third Reich. This was not only the case with King Leopold and Marshal Pétain; there was a moment when many, perhaps most, of the elected parliamentary representatives of Holland and Belgium and Denmark and, of course, the French Republic were moving in that direction. That state of affairs would soon — at the latest by October 1940 — pass, because England was holding out, because of Churchill. His phrases about London having become the custodian of Western civilization were not mere rhetoric: there was the presence of the exiled kings and queens of Western Europe in its mansions, there was the colorful presence of their uniformed soldiers and sailors in its streets (including the brave Poles, thousands of them); there were those Bach concerts in its darkened Victorian halls — and the British Broadcasting Corporation's signal opening its European broadcasts with the first bar of Beethoven's Fifth Symphony.

A half-century later a new generation of Churchill's critics has appeared, some of them critical of his vision, some of his resolution, some of both. Eschewing extreme or pro-Nazi representatives, we have the works of such professional historians as Maurice Cowling or David Reynolds or Sheila Lawlor or John Charmley (the latter enthusiastically supported by Alan Clark). This is not the place to describe or analyze their writings in detail, but the essence of their revisionist criticism may be summed up as follows: that Churchill had no plan in May 1940 except to keep fighting, hoping that something might turn up (Micawber-like), though he hardly knew what;[45] and that Churchill's obsessive hatred of Hitler may have blinded him, for had he accepted an accommodation with Hitler by 1941 at the latest, the Empire might have been saved. This argument has been presented, too, by certain German historians, especially Andreas Hillgruber,[46] who was determined to argue that Churchill's principal aim was the destruction not only of Hitler but of Germany, an unconscionable imperialist policy with lamentable results. That many Germans have no liking for Churchill may be understandable. But is it justifiable? Who else stood in Hitler's way in 1940 — and

45. Examples from Sheila Lawlor (an estimable historian) in her *Churchill and the Politics of War:* "John Charmley's provocative biography . . . has been taken by supporters and detractors alike to remove the trappings of myth which Churchill wove around his own conduct. But for the early years of the war, the treatment is uncontroversial" (18). "Trappings of myth": perhaps. "Uncontroversial": no. Lawlor continues: Churchill "was helped by events themselves — the fall of France, Holland, and Belgium and the attack on Britain herself — and by his own reaction to them. His earlier characteristics of reaction and bombast . . . " (43). Two different reactions? "Churchill's decision to fight on was more reasonable and had more in common with that of Chamberlain and Halifax than his rhetoric might suggest, but it was his rhetoric which, in the summer of 1940, had begun to cast him into his wartime caricature" (87). Caricature? Image, rather: for an image is not independent from reality, whereas a caricature is but a part of it. About Chamberlain, she says: "Churchill, though insisting there should be no scapegoats, that all were equally responsible, that they were 'all guilty' — nonetheless did not stop the critics" (89). Yes, he did: and the result was most beneficial for his relationship with Chamberlain.

46. Hillgruber, a principal German historian of the Second World War, wrote in his massive and important book *Hitlers Strategie,* 144 n. 1, that "from his viewpoint" Hitler's offers to Britain were "seriously meant" and "subjectively, honest."

who was committed to the restoration of law and democracy in Western Europe, including Germany?

♦ ♦ ♦

I began this last chapter, entitled "Survival," with this sentence: "Had Hitler won the Second World War we would be living in a different world." And now, at the end of this chapter, indeed of this small book, I must change its tone and end with a fortissimo. At the end of May 1940 and for some time thereafter, not only the end of a European war but the end of Western civilization was near. Churchill knew that, inspired as he was by a kind of historical consciousness that entailed more than incantatory rhetoric. Here are two examples. On 31 May, when he had flown to Paris and had impressed at least Reynaud by the strength of his resolution, he also said, near the end of their meeting: "If Germany defeated either ally or both, she would give no mercy; we should be reduced to the status of vassals *forever.* It would be better far that the civilisation of Western Europe with all of its achievements should come to a tragic but splendid end than that the two great democracies should linger on, stripped of all that made life worth living." Nineteen days later, when France fell, he struck the same tone and theme. If Hitler wins and we fall, he said, "then the whole world, including the United States, including all that we have known and care for, will sink into the abyss of a New Dark Age, made more sinister, and perhaps more *protracted,* by the lights of perverted science."

These italics are mine. Churchill understood something that not many people understand even now. The greatest threat to Western civilization was not Communism. It was National Socialism. The greatest and most dynamic power in the world was not Soviet Russia. It was the Third Reich of Germany. The greatest revolutionary of the twentieth century was not Lenin or Stalin. It was Hitler.

Hitler not only succeeded in merging nationalism and socialism into one tremendous force; he was a new kind of ruler, representing a new kind of populist nationalism. What was more, the remnants of the older order (or disorder) were not capable of withstanding him; indeed, some of their conservative representatives, in Germany and elsewhere, were inclined — for many reasons, including their fear of Communism — to accommodate themselves to him. It was thus that in 1940 he represented a wave of the future.[47] His greatest reactionary opponent, Churchill, was like King Canute, attempting to withstand and sweep back that wave. And — yes, *mirabile dictu* — this King Canute succeeded: because of his resolution and — allow me to say this — because of God's will, of which, like every human being, he was but an instrument. He was surely no saint, he was not a religious man, and he had many faults. Yet so it happened.

Had Hitler won, his New Order, too, would not have lasted forever, though it might have lasted for a long time. In 1989 I wrote a book about the duel between Churchill and Hitler in 1940. Now, ten years later, we can see that in 1989 not only was an entire century closing (the short twentieth century from 1914 to 1989) but an entire age was closing as well, an age that had begun about five hundred years ago and that was, among other things, characterized by the struggle and increasing coexistence of Aristocracy with Democracy, with the latter gradually rising and the former gradually weakening. Now we have begun living in an age where the remnants of that earlier age are gone and when global democracy — unques-

---

47. "I could hear this drumming coming right through the earth," Enoch Powell later recalled. "Powell could see that Hitler was bent on war; worse, he thought that the Nazis would win," writes Derek Turner in "A Valediction for Enoch Powell," *Chronicles* (November 1998). (Powell had a fine war record; he became the youngest brigadier in the British army.)

tioned democracy, with its unforeseeable circumstances and conditions and perils — is beginning. This is neither the place nor the time to speculate about that. But what we must understand is that the history of the fifty years from 1940 to 1990 was inseparable from what happened in 1940, just as the Cold War too was but the result of the Second World War. At best, civilization may survive, at least in some small part due to Churchill in 1940. At worst, he helped to give us — especially those of us who are no longer young but who were young then — fifty years. Fifty years before the rise of new kinds of barbarism not incarnated by the armed might of Germans or Russians, before the clouds of a new Dark Age may darken the lives of our children and grandchildren. Fifty years! Perhaps that was enough.

Bibliography

Unpublished Sources

PUBLIC RECORD OFFICE, LONDON/KEW

CAB 65 War Cabinet Conclusions and Confidential Annexes
CAB 66 War Cabinet Memoranda
CAB 69 Defence Committee and Confidential Annex
CAB 99 Supreme War Council Meetings
CAB 127 Private Office Papers (Horace Wilson)
PREM 3 Prime Minister's Papers
PREM 4 Prime Minister's Papers
WO 216 Chief of the Imperial General Staff
INF Ministry of Information Papers
FO 371 Foreign Office Papers
FO 408 Foreign Office Papers
FO 800 (800/323 Halifax, 800/326 Mallet) Foreign Office Papers
FO 1011 Foreign Office Papers

Bibliography

CHURCHILL ARCHIVES, CHURCHILL COLLEGE, CAMBRIDGE
(CA AND CH/A)

1/355 1940 Correspondence
2/394–401 1940 Personal Office
20/1/8 Correspondence
22/3 Cabinet Notes and Correspondence
Chartwell Household Papers
Churchill: Private Correspondence
Cadogan, Sir Alexander, Diaries
Colville, John, Diaries
Cooper, Alfred Duff, Earl of Norwich, Diaries and Papers
Halifax, Earl of, Papers, Microfilmed. (Also see below, in York.)
Hankey, Lord Maurice, Diaries and Papers
Jacob, Sir Ian, Diaries
Margesson, Viscount David, Diaries
Reeves (Emery: Révész) Papers
Vansittart, Sir Robert, Diaries

OTHER UNPUBLISHED SOURCES

Alanbrooke, Viscount (Sir Alan Francis Brooke). Papers. King's College, London.
Astor, Nancy. Papers. University of Reading.
Butler, R. A. Papers. Trinity College, Cambridge.
Chamberlain, Neville. Papers. University of Birmingham.
Dalton, Hugh. Papers. London School of Economics.
Eden, Anthony (Earl of Avon). Papers. University of Birmingham.
Esnouf, G. N. "British Government War Aims and Attitudes Toward a Negotiated Peace, September 1939 to July 1940." Ph.D. diss., Cambridge, 1988. In the Library of King's College, London.
Halifax, Earl of. Papers. Borthwick Institute, University of York.
Ismay, Lord Hastings. Papers. King's College, London.
Lawlor, Sheila. "British Policies and Strategy, May 1940–March 1941." Ph.D. diss., Cambridge, 1980.

Bibliography

Lloyd George, David. Papers. House of Lords Record Office, London.
Mass-Observation Archives. University of Sussex, Falmer/Brighton.
Nicolson, Harold. Papers. Balliol College, Oxford.

Published Sources

DOCUMENTARY COLLECTIONS

ADAP *Akten zur deutschen auswärtigen Politik, 1918–1945,* series D, vols. 10, 11. Frankfurt and Bonn, 1961–65.
AOK/KTB *Armeeoberkommando/Kriegstagebuch des Oberkommandos der Wehrmacht.* P. Schramm, ed. Frankfurt, 1961–65.
BBC/WAC BBC Written Archives Centre. Caversham Park, Reading.
Churchill and Roosevelt: The Complete Correspondence, vol. 1. W. Kimball, ed. Princeton, 1985.
The Churchill War Papers. Companion Volume 2. Martin Gilbert, ed. New York, 1995.
DDI *Documenti diplomatici italiani, 1939–1943,* series 9, vol. 4. Rome, 1965.
Hansard House of Commons Record of Sessions.
Hitler, Adolf. *The Testament of Adolf Hitler: The Hitler-Bormann Documents, February–April 1945.* London, 1959.

DIARIES AND MEMOIRS

Allingham, Margery. *The Oaken Heart.* New York, 1941.
Amery, Leo. *My Political Life,* vol. 2. London, 1955.
——. *The Empire at Bay: The Leo Amery Diaries, 1929–1945.* London, 1988.
Among You Taking Notes: The Wartime Diary of Naomi Mitchison, 1939–1945. Dorothy Sheridan, ed. London, 1985.
Baffy: The Diaries of Blanche Dugdale, 1936–1947. Norman Rose, ed. London, 1967.
Boothby, Robert. *I Fight to Live.* London, 1967.
Brittain, Vera. *England's Hour.* New York, 1941.
The Diaries of Sir Alexander Cadogan. David Dilks, ed. London, 1971.
Chips: The Diaries of Sir Henry Channon. Robert James Rhodes, ed. London, 1967.

Clark, Kenneth. *Another Part of the Wood: A Self-Portrait.* New York, 1974.

Colville, John. *The Fringes of Power: Downing Street Diaries, 1939–1945.* London, 1985.

Cooper, Duff. *Old Men Forget.* London, 1953.

Dalton, Hugh. *The Fateful Years: Memoirs, 1939–1945.* London, 1957.

———. *The Second World War Diary of Hugh Dalton, 1940–1945.* Ben Pimlott, ed. London, 1988.

de Gaulle, Charles. *The Call to Honour, 1940–1942.* Vol. 1 of *War Memoirs.* London, 1955.

Eden, Anthony. *The Reckoning.* London, 1965.

Engel, D. *Heeresadjutant bei Hitler, 1938–1943,* Stuttgart, 1974.

Forrestal, James. *The Forrestal Diaries.* Walter Millis, ed. New York, 1951.

Halder, F. *Kriegstagebuch, 1939–1942.* H. Jacobsen, ed. Stuttgart, 1962.

Halifax, Earl of. *Fulness of Days.* London, 1957.

The Diplomatic Diaries of Oliver Harvey. London, 1970.

Henrey, Mrs. Robert. *The Siege of London.* London, 1946.

Hewison, Robert. *Under Siege: Literary Life in London, 1939–1945.* London, 1988.

Ironside, William Edmund. *The Ironside Diaries, 1937–1940.* Roderick Macleod and Denis Kelly, eds. London, 1962.

Ismay, Lord Hastings. *The Memoirs of Lord Ismay.* London, 1960.

With Malice Toward None: A War Diary by Cecil H. King. W. Armstrong, ed. London, 1970.

Macmillan, Harold. *The Blast of War, 1939–1945.* New York, 1967.

Milburn's Diary: An Englishwoman's Daily Reflections, 1939–1945. Peter Donnelly, ed. London, 1979.

Nella's Last War: A Mother's Diary, 1939–1945. Richard Broad and Suzie Fleming, eds. London, 1981.

Nicolson, Harold. *1939–1945.* Vol. 2 of *Diaries and Letters.* Nigel Nicolson, ed. London, 1967.

The Collected Essays, Journalism, and Letters of George Orwell: 1940–1943. Sonia Orwell and Ian Angus, eds. London 1968.

Chief of Staff: The Diaries of Lieutenant General Henry Pownall. 2 vols. Brian Bond, ed. London, 1972, 1975.

Raczynski, Edward. *In Wartime London.* London, 1962.

Bibliography

Reith, Lord. *The Reith Diaries*. Stuart Charles, ed. London, 1975.

Schroeder, Christa. *Er War mein Chef: Aus den Nachlass der Sekretärin von Adolf Hitler*. A. Joachimsthaler, ed. Munich, 1985.

Thompson, W. H. *Fifty Minutes with Winston Churchill*. London, 1951.

The Diaries of Evelyn Waugh. Michael Davie, ed. London, 1976.

Woolf, Leonard. *The Journey Not the Arrival Matters: An Autobiography of the Years, 1939–1969*. New York, 1970

The Diary of Virginia Woolf. Vol. 5. New York, 1984.

OTHER PUBLISHED SOURCES

Addison, Paul. *The Road to 1945: British Politics and the Second World War*. London, 1975.

———. "Churchill in British Politics, 1940–1955." In *The Political Culture of Modern Britain: Studies in Memory of Stephen Koss*. J. M. W. Bean, ed. London, 1987.

Ansel, W. *Hitler Confronts England*. Durham, N.C., 1960.

Aster, Sidney. *The Making of the Second World War*. London, 1939, 1973.

Bell, P. M. H. *A Certain Eventuality: Britain and the Fall of France*. London, 1974.

———. "British Public Opinion on the War and the French Alliance, September 1939–May 1940." English typescript of his article in *Français et britanniques dans la drôle de guerre* (1979): 51–80.

Birkenhead, Earl of. *Halifax: The Life of Lord Halifax*. London, 1965.

Bond, Brian. *Britain, France, and Belgium, 1939–1940*. London, 1975.

Calder, Angus. *The People's War: Britain, 1939–1945*. London, 1969.

Cannadine, David C. *Aspects of Aristocracy*. New Haven, 1994.

Charmley, John. *Churchill: The End of Glory*. London, 1993.

Churchill, Winston Spencer. *Their Finest Hour*. Vol. 2 of *The Second World War*. Boston, 1949.

Colvin, Ian. *The Chamberlain Cabinet: How the Meetings in 10 Downing Street, 1937–9, Led to the Second World War*. London, 1971.

Cowling, Maurice. *The Impact of Hitler: British Politics and British Policy, 1933–1940*. Cambridge, 1975.

Delpla, François. *Les Papiers secrets de général Doumenc*. Paris, 1992.

———. *La Ruse nazie: Dunkerque, 24 mai 1940*. Paris, 1992.

Bibliography

Dilks, David. "Allied Leadership in the Second World War: Churchill." *Survey* 21, nos. 1/2 (1975).

———. "The Twilight War and the Fall of France: Chamberlain and Churchill in 1940." *Transactions of the Royal Historical Society,* 5th series, vol. 28 (1978): 61–86.

Feiling, Keith. *The Life of Neville Chamberlain.* London, 1946, 1970.

Gates, Eleanor M. *The End of the Affair: The Collapse of the Anglo-French Alliance, 1939–1940.* Berkeley, 1981.

Gilbert, Martin. *Finest Hour, 1939–1941.* Vol. 6 of *Winston S. Churchill.* Boston, 1983.

Gillam, Geoffrey. *Enfield at War, 1939–1945.* n.d.

Green, Henry. *Caught.* London, 1943.

Hillgruber, Andreas. *Hitlers Strategie: Politik und Kriegsführung, 1940–1941.* Düsseldorf, 1965.

Howard, Anthony. RAB: *The Life of R. A. Butler.* London, 1987.

Howard, Michael. *The Continental Commitment: The Dilemma of British Defence Policy in the Era of the Two World Wars.* London, 1972.

Keyes, Sir Roger. *Outrageous Fortune: The Tragedy of Leopold II of the Belgians, 1901–1941.* London, 1984.

Lamb, Richard. *The Ghosts of Peace, 1935–1945.* London, 1987.

Lawlor, Sheila. *Churchill and the Politics of War, 1940–1941.* Cambridge, 1994.

Lukacs, John. *The Last European War, 1939–1941.* New York, 1976.

———. *The Duel: 10 May–31 July 1940; The Eighty-Day Struggle Between Churchill and Hitler.* New York, 1991.

Mass-Observation. *War Begins at Home.* London, 1940.

Mortimer, John, *Clinging to the Wreckage.* New York, 1982.

Moynihan, Michael, ed. *People at War, 1939–1942.* London, 1972.

Neave, Airey. *The Flames of Calais.* London, 1972.

Ponting, Clive. *1940: Myth and Reality.* London, 1990.

Powell, Anthony. *A Dance to the Music of Time,* vols. 7 and 8. London, 1964, 1966.

Raleigh, Sir Walter. *English Voyages of the Sixteenth Century.* Glasgow, 1928.

Reynolds, David. "Churchill and the British Decision to Fight On in 1940: Right Policy, Wrong Reasons." In *Diplomacy and Intelligence.* R. Langhorne, ed. Cambridge, 1985.

———. *The Creation of the Anglo-American Alliance, 1937–1941*. London, 1989.

———. "1940: Fulcrum of the Twentieth Century?" *International Affairs,* 66 (1990).

Roberts, Andrew. *The Holy Fox: A Life of Lord Halifax*. London, 1991.

———. *Eminent Churchillians*. London, 1994.

Rose, Kenneth. *King George V.* New York, 1984.

Simpson, A. W. B. *In the Highest Degree Odious: Detention Without Trial in Wartime Britain*. London, 1992.

Smith, Godfrey, ed. *The English Reader: An Anthology*. London, 1988.

Taylor, A. J. P. *English History, 1914–1945*, Oxford, 1965.

Villelume, P. *Journal d'une défaite*. Paris, 1976.

War Begins at Home: Mass-Observation. London, 1940.

Wheeler-Bennett, Sir John. *King George VI*. London, 1958.

———. *Action This Day: Working with Churchill*. Memoirs by Lord Normanbrook, John Colville, Sir John Martin, Sir Ian Jacob, Lord Bridges, and Sir Leslie Rowan. London, 1968.

Woodward, Sir Llewellyn. *History of the Second World War: British Foreign Policy in the Second World War.* 2 vols. London, 1971.

Ziegler, Philip. *London at War, 1939–1945*. New York, 1995.

NEWSPAPERS (23–30 MAY 1940)

Daily Express
Daily Herald
Daily Mail
Daily Mirror
Daily Telegraph
Illustrated London News
Manchester Guardian
News Chronicle
The Scotsman
Times (London)
Yorkshire Post

Illustration Credits

Page 28 — AP / Wide World Photos. Reprinted by permission.

Page 36 — From the archives of the Imperial War Museum, London. Reprinted by permission of the Trustees of the Imperial War Museum, London.

Page 52 — Ian Colvin, *The Chamberlain Cabinet* (New York, 1971), frontispiece.

Page 70 — AP/Wide World Photos. Reprinted by permission.

Page 154 — Private collection of the Earl of Halifax, reprinted in Andrew Roberts, *The Holy Fox: A Life of Lord Halifax* (London, 1991), 108.

Page 166 — *Punch,* 14 August 1940. Reprinted by permission.

Page 176 — Photograph from PopperFoto / Archives Photo. Reprinted by permission.

Index

Index

Index

Index

Mass Observation (M.-O.), 34 ff., 80–81, 102–3, 160–61, 165–66, 198, 213
Medlicott, W. N., 107n.
Ministry of Information, 100, 132
Molinié, General, 139
Molotov, V. M., 170
Montgomery, Bernard Law, 196
Morand, Paul, 172n.
Morrison, Herbert, 184
Mosley, Sir Oswald, 5, 81, 89, 129, 183
Muggeridge, Malcolm, 30, 83n.
Mussolini, Benito, 8, 15, 54, 85, 110 ff., 114–15, 120n., 125, 146 ff., 158, 172, 182, 193, 205

Neave, Airey, 20, 44–45
News Chronicle, 76, 79, 99, 159, 169–70, 197
New Zealand, 75
Nicholson, Claude, 20, 43, 45–46, 97, 129
Nicolson, Harold, 131, 157, 158n., 168–69, 198
Nordling, 88n.
Norway, 12, 88n.

Orwell, George, 30, 86n., 158n., 167–68, 171n., 209–10

Pascal, Blaise, 29, 31
Percival, A. E., 42
Perowne, Stewart, 21n.

Pétain, Philippe, 53, 77, 86–87, 111, 203, 215
Phillimore, Lord, 91
Poland, 11–12
Powell, Anthony, 30
Powell, Enoch, 218n.
Pownall, Henry, 17, 23–24, 43n., 44n., 50n., 54n., 174, 202, 208–9
Prioux, General, 139
Prytz, Björn, 203

Raczynski, Edward, 173
Ramsey, Sir Bertram, 137
Reynaud, Paul, 77, 86, 105, 111 ff., 130, 147 ff., 181–82, 192, 216
Reynolds, David, 127, 157n., 215
Ribbentrop, Joachim von, 63n., 69n.
Roberts, Andrew, 19n., 21n., 50, 57n., 60, 66, 94–95, 123, 127, 151n., 155n., 185, 186n., 214n.
Roosevelt, Eleanor, 72n.
Roosevelt, Franklin D., 53, 71 ff., 118, 143–44, 157n., 172, 188, 206–7
Rundstedt, Karl, 34 ff., 192
Russia, 29, 51, 80, 90, 168–69, 214

Sargent, Sir Orme, 186n.
Schacht, Hjalmar, 51
Schroeder, Christa, 41n.
Schuschnigg, Kurt von, 59

Index